30 DAYS TO THE

New GED

30 One-Day Lessons for Complete GED Prep

Nathan Barber

THOMSON
ARCO

Australia • Canada • Mexico • Singapore • Spain • United Kingdom • United States

About The Author

Nathan Barber has authored a number of test-preparation books in a variety of fields and has served as an expert reviewer. Barber currently teaches at a college preparatory school in Texas where he has worked with students to prepare them for standardized tests and college courses for more than five years. Barber currently resides in Texas with his wife, Christy, and son, Noah.

THE 30-DAY PROGRAM

CREDITS

Day 1 to Day 18

Preparing for the GED

Day 1

Introduction to the GED

Topics for today:

1. What is the GED?
2. History of the GED
3. The GED Test Areas
4. How to use this book
5. What you should do next

1. WHAT IS THE GED?

The Tests of General Education Development, or GED, are standardized tests that measure skills required of high school graduates in the United States and in Canada. These skills are in four areas, including Language Arts, Social Studies, Science, and Mathematics. In order to receive a passing score, a test candidate must demonstrate a mastery of skills in those areas at least equal to the top two thirds of high school graduates. Candidates who pass the GED will receive a diploma or a diploma equivalent.

Many times each year, the GED Testing Service of the American Council on Education administers the tests throughout the United States and Canada and offers the tests in English, French, Spanish, large print, Braille, and even audio tape format. To learn more about when and where the GED will be administered in your area, contact the GED Testing Service:

General Educational Development
GED Testing Service
American Council on Education
One Dupont Circle, NW
Washington, DC 20036
800-626-9433 (toll-free)
www.gedtest.org

2. HISTORY OF THE GED

The GED Tests were created originally for veterans of World War II whose education had been interrupted by the war. The GED Tests gave the veterans an opportunity to complete their educations after they returned from the war. Since the 1940s, the focus of the tests has shifted toward men and women like you who want to earn their high school diplomas, fulfill job requirements, or fulfill college entrance requirements in order to continue their education. One example of such a change is the increase in adult-context information throughout the tests.

One thing has not changed, though. Millions of motivated men and women like you have earned their high school credentials by completing GED Tests.

3. THE GED TEST AREAS

The GED Tests cover the four core areas of the traditional high school curriculum: Language Arts, Social Studies, Mathematics, and Science. Let's take a brief look at each of the areas that will be tested on the GED.

The Language Arts portion of the GED is divided into two sections: Language Arts, Writing and Language Arts, Reading. The Language Arts, Writing Test has two parts—a multiple-choice section and an essay—but you will receive only a single score for the test. The multiple-choice section contains several passages and questions about those passages in which you find errors or determine the best way to rewrite particular sentences. Basically, the multiple-choice section tests English grammar and usage. The essay section will require you to write a 200 to 250 word essay on a particular topic. You will be expected to demonstrate skills in grammar, usage, sentence structure, and organization. In addition, you will be asked to draw on your knowledge and life experience to answer the essay.

The Social Studies Test contains multiple-choice questions in the areas of history, economics, political science, and geography. In the United States, the test will focus on U.S. history and government, while the test in Canada will focus on Canadian history and government. World history will be included to some extent, too. The questions measure your skills in comprehension, analysis, application, and evaluation within the context of the Social Studies areas.

Like the Social Studies Test, the Science Test contains multiple-choice questions that measure comprehension, analysis, application, and evaluation. These skills are measured within the context of both physical and life sciences. You also can expect to see some aspects of earth science, space science, life science, health science, and environmental science on the Science Test.

Like the Language Arts Test, the Mathematics Test contains two parts. Part I permits the use of a calculator, and Part II does not; you will be given time before the test to practice with the calculator in case you are unfamiliar with the particular model used. The Mathematics Test measures skills in algebra, geometry, data analysis, statistics, and problem solving.

4. HOW TO USE THIS BOOK

This book has been designed with you, the adult test taker, in mind. Your success on the GED Tests is the one and only goal of this book. Therefore, this book will serve as an invaluable tool during the time in which you prepare for the GED. It is important that you work through this book in order, beginning with Day 1 and ending with Day 30. You can always go back and review chapters that you have already done, but don't work ahead or skip around in the book. One of the best ways to make the most of the time spent in review with this book is to develop a routine. Ideally, you should get into a routine that allows you 30–60 minutes of uninterrupted study time each day. Some people work best in the morning, while others perform well at night. Decide what works best for you and stick with it. Many educational researchers also recommend that you study at the same time and in the same place each day. If this is possible, you should make every effort to do so.

As you work through this book, remember that this book is a guide to help sharpen the skills that you already possess. The GED does not test random facts and trivial information. The GED measures practical, useful skills, most of which you probably use everyday whether you realize it or not. This book will help you turn those skills into success on the GED Tests.

5. WHAT TO DO NEXT

The fact that you are reading this book indicates that you have taken the first step toward passing the GED Tests. But what should you do next? If you have not already registered for the GED, you should make some contacts right away. Also, if you would like to enroll in a GED test-preparation course or program in addition to working through this book and others in the ARCO line of books, you need to make contacts as soon as possible. If you don't know when and were the tests are administered or if you don't know where to enroll in a test-prep course, begin by calling your local high school counselor. You might also call the Adult Education or Continuing Education Department at your local community college, college, or university. The people in those offices can either give you the information you need or they can direct you to the person or persons with whom you need to speak.

Day 2

What to Expect on the GED

Topics for today:

1. General types of questions on the GED Tests
2. The focus of the questions on each subject area test

1. GENERAL TYPES OF QUESTIONS ON THE GED TESTS

On the GED Tests, you can expect to see only two question formats, multiple choice and essay. On every test except for Language Arts, Writing, all the questions will be multiple choice. Each multiple-choice question will have five possible answer choices. For each question, you are to choose the best answer of the five possible choices. The multiple-choice questions, which are discussed in great detail on Day 3, may be based on a graphic, a text, or a mathematics problem, or they may just test your knowledge of a particular subject. The other type of question you can expect to see on the GED is the essay question. As mentioned above, the Language Arts, Writing Test, in addition to some multiple-choice questions, will have a question of a different sort. On the Language Arts, Writing Test, you will have the opportunity to write a 45-minute essay on a topic that is given to you. There will be no surprises for you on the GED and the format will not vary from that which you just learned.

That should help you relax as you take the test because you know exactly what kinds of questions to expect.

2. THE FOCUS OF THE QUESTIONS ON EACH SUBJECT AREA TEST

Let's take a brief look at the focus of the questions on each subject area test. The lessons in Days 11–17 will take you step by step through every aspect of each subject area test. Today, though, you will learn about the questions on each subject area test. Let's start with the Language Arts, Writing Test. Part I of Language Arts, Writing will be multiple-choice questions that cover grammar and usage. As you know, this test will also require you to write a 45-minute essay of about 250 or so words. This question will not test your knowledge of a particular subject, such as the War of 1812 or the Pythagorean Theorem. Rather, the question will give you a chance to write an essay that draws upon your experiences. The readers of the essay will not be grading the essay based on how much you know or don't know about the topic but rather on how well you use standard English.

The Social Studies Test, like all the remaining tests, will be in multiple-choice format. The Social Studies questions will be presented in a variety of ways and will test a variety of skills. Some of the questions will be based on reading passages, and some questions will be based on graphics such as maps, charts, illustrations, or political cartoons. You will learn how to attack these types of questions on Days 8–10. Some of the questions will be in sets. In other words, you may read a passage and then answer two or more questions based on that passage. Some of the questions will be single items, or a single question about a graphic or a reading passage. The questions will be worded so that the Social Studies Test measures skills such as comprehension of information, application of information and concepts, analysis of information or data, and evaluation of information and concepts. All of these skills are covered in Days 4–7. You will learn about the Social Studies subject area information on Day 13.

The Science Test also uses multiple-choice questions to test your knowledge and skills. As with the Social Studies Test, some of the Science questions will be based upon reading passages and some of the questions will be based upon graphics such as scientific diagrams. The Science Test will also ask you a few questions to test your general knowledge of science and scientific principles. You can expect to see more single items and fewer sets on the Science Test. You will learn about the Science subject area information on Day 14.

The Language Arts, Reading Test is similar to the Social Studies and Science Tests in that the multiple-choice questions will be based on passages. However, there are no graphics in the Language Arts, Reading Test. The questions will be based on longer passages than questions in the other subject area tests. In the Language Arts, Reading Test, some of the questions will be based on a poem, some on prose, and some on a piece of drama. These questions will not measure your ability to critique literature. Rather, they will measure your analysis and synthesis skills and your comprehension and appli-

cation skills. You will learn about the Language Arts, Reading subject area information on Day 15.

The Mathematics Test uses multiple-choice questions to measure your skills in arithmetic, algebra, geometry, and problem solving. Some of the questions will ask you to find the answer to a problem, while others will require you to find the best way to solve the problem. Many of the questions will be based upon diagrams. Some of the questions will be grouped into sets that require you to drawn upon information from a number of sources, such as graphs and charts. You will learn about the Mathematics subject area information on Days 16 and 17.

As you read the paragraphs above, you may have noticed that the majority of the questions throughout the tests are intended to measure your skills and test-taking abilities, while relatively few questions test the limits of your knowledge. What does this mean for you? This means that if you work hard to sharpen your test-taking skills and you master the approaches presented in this book, you are much more prepared for success on the tests than if you sat down and memorized names, dates, facts, properties, charts, or other bits of information. Basically, you will have more success on the GED if you know how to take the tests than if you all you know is information about reading, writing, science, social studies, and math. Now that you have a general idea of what to expect on the GED Tests, let's start learning how to master the skills necessary for success on the GED.

Day 3

Answering Multiple-Choice Questions

Topics for today:

1. Understanding general multiple-choice questions
2. Understanding multiple-choice questions on the GED Tests
3. Strategies for attacking multiple-choice questions

1. UNDERSTANDING GENERAL MULTIPLE-CHOICE QUESTIONS

For years, students and test takers have been taking multiple-choice tests, and for years, students and test takers have had two significant misconceptions about multiple-choice tests. On the one hand, many test takers believe that multiple-choice tests are very easy and require no preparation at all. Those test takers usually believe that multiple-choice strategy simply amounts to picking the correct answer out of a lineup. In addition, these same test takers believe that simple knowledge, with no comprehension, is all that is needed for success on multiple-choice tests. On the other hand, many test takers believe that multiple-choice tests are the hardest of all possible tests to master. Those test takers usually believe this because of the misconception that the test creators are out to trick and confuse test takers. The bottom line is that these ideas are misconceptions and that multiple-choice questions are very manageable.

The key to success on multiple-choice tests is understanding the questions and how to find the cor-

rect answer. With good strategy, you will be able to handle any multiple-choice question that you encounter, even on tests other than the GED and even questions for which you don't necessarily know the answer. The construction of multiple-choice questions varies very little from test to test. The question, also known as the stem or question stem, is always followed by a few or several possible answer choices. In some cases, there is only one choice that could possibly answer the question correctly. In other cases, there may be two or more choices that might be somewhat correct; in cases like this, one choice will be the best choice. The number of answer choices may vary from test to test, but all multiple-choice questions are basically the same.

2. UNDERSTANDING THE MULTIPLE-CHOICE QUESTIONS ON THE GED TESTS

As you learned in previous lessons, all questions on the GED Tests are—with the exception of the essay question on the Language Arts, Writing Test—in multiple-choice format. Each question will be followed by five answer choices: 1,2,3,4, and 5. There will be no trick questions and no questions intended to confuse you. If you use the strategies that follow, you will be very successful on the multiple-choice questions.

3. STRATEGIES FOR ATTACKING MULTIPLE-CHOICE QUESTIONS

Read the question carefully and make sure you know what the question is asking. Read each question slowly. If you rush through the question, you might miss a key word that could cost you the correct answer. You might want to run your pencil under the question as you read it to be sure that you don't miss anything in the question. If you don't understand the question after the first time you read it, go back and read the question another time or two until you do understand it.

Don't over-analyze the question or read something into the question that just isn't there. Many test takers make the mistake of over-analyzing the questions, looking for some trick or hidden meaning that the test creators added for the sake of confusion. The GED Test creators didn't do that at all on any of the questions, so take each question at face value. Each question will say exactly what it means, so don't try to read something unusual into the questions.

Circle or underline the key words in the question. As you read through the question, locate any important words in the question and either circle or underline the word or words. Important words will be anything taken directly from the chart, table, graph, or reading passage on which the question is based. Other important words will be words like *compare*, *contrast*, *similar*, *different*, or *main idea*. By circling or underlining the key words, you will understand the question better and will be more prepared to recognize the correct answer.

After you read the question, try to answer the question in your head before you look at the answer choices. If you think you know the answer to the question without even looking at the answer choices, then you most likely will recognize the correct answer right away when you read the possible answer choices. Also, if you think you know the correct answer right away, then you should be very confident in your answer when you find it listed among the possible answer choices.

Try covering the answer choices while you are reading the question. To try answering the question in your head without being influenced by the answer choices, cover the answer choices with your hand as you read the question. This technique will also help prevent you from reading something into the question that isn't there based on something you saw in one of the answer choices first. Covering the answer choices may also help you concentrate only on the question to make sure you read it carefully and correctly.

Carefully read all the answer choices before answering the question. You need to look at all the possibilities before you choose the best or correct answer. Even if you think you know the answer before looking at the possible answer choices, read all of the answer choices anyway. If you read through two of the answer choices and you find that choice (3) is a good answer, keep reading because (4) or (5) may very well be a better answer. Finally, by reading all the answer choices, you can be more confident in your answer because you will see that the others are definitely incorrect.

Eliminate answer choices that you know are wrong. As you read through all the choices, some of the answer choices will obviously be incorrect. When you find those answer choices, mark through them. This will help you narrow the possible choices. In addition, marking through incorrect answers will prevent you from choosing an incorrect answer by mistake.

Don't spend too much time on one question. If you read a question and you just can't seem to find the best or correct answer, circle the question, skip it, and come back to it later. Your time will be better spent answering questions that you can answer. Your time is limited, so don't spend the time struggling with one question that you could devote to correctly answering three others.

Go with your first answer. Once you choose an answer, be confident in your answer and stick to it. Statistics from numerous studies have shown that a test taker's first hunch is usually the correct one. There is a reason why your brain told you to choose a particular answer, so stand by it. Also, don't waste time debating over whether the answer you chose is correct. Go with your first answer and move on.

Don't go back and change your answer unless you have a good, solid reason to do so. Remember that your first hunch is usually the best, so don't change your answer on a whim. One of the only times you should change your answer on a previous question is if you find something later in the test that is concrete and contradicts what you chose. The only other time you should change an answer is if you remember very clearly a teacher's lecture, a reading passage, or some other reliable source of information to the contrary of what you chose.

Look for hints within the answer choices. For example, some sets of answer choices may contain two choices that vary by only a word or two. Chances are that the correct answer is one of those two answers.

Watch out for descriptive words and absolutes. Other hints within answer choices can be words called absolutes. These words include *always*, *never*, *only*, or *completely*. These words severely limit the possibility of that answer choice being right because the absolutes make answer choices that include them correct under certain, very limited circumstances.

If you just don't know the correct answer, guess. That's right, guess. The GED Tests are scored based on how many questions you answer correctly, and there is no point penalty for answering incorrectly. Therefore, why leave questions unanswered? If you do, you have no chance at getting points for those. However, if you guess, you at least have a chance to get some points. Before you guess, try to eliminate as many wrong answer choices as possible if you haven't already done so. Let's look at an example. If you guess on a question and you have not eliminated any incorrect answers, you have a 1 in 5 chance of choosing the correct answer. If you can eliminate two incorrect answers, you have a 1 in 4

chance. If you can eliminate three, you have a 1 in 3 chance, and so on. The fact is that you have a much greater chance of choosing the correct answer if you can weed out some that are incorrect. This strategy is especially helpful if you have several questions left for which you are going to guess.

Be aware of how much time you have left on the test. However, don't glance down at your watch or up at the clock after every question to check the time. You will be instructed at the beginning of the test as to the amount of time you have to complete the test. Just be aware of that amount of time. The creators of the GED Tests designed the tests and the test times so that you will have ample time to complete the tests. As you approach the point at which you have 10 minutes left, make sure that you are not spending your time answering the difficult questions if you still have other questions ahead of you that you can answer. If you have answered all the questions that you can with relatively little difficulty, go back and work on those that gave you trouble. If you come down to the wire and have a few left, guess at the answers. There is no penalty for wrong answers on the GED.

If you have time left at the end of the test, go back to any questions that you skipped. As you just read, after you finish all the questions that you can without too much difficulty, you should go back over the test and find the ones you skipped. The amount of time you have left should determine the amount of time you spend on each unanswered question. For example, if you have 10 questions left and 10 minutes left, try to work on a few of them. However, if you have 10 questions left and 2 minutes left, go through and guess on each of the remaining questions.

Before you take the practice tests in this book, you may want to glance back over these strategies so that you can make the most of your multiple-choice practice experience.

Day 4

Answering Comprehension Questions

Topics for today:

1. What is Bloom's Taxonomy?
2. Understanding comprehension questions
3. Practicing comprehension questions

1. WHAT IS BLOOM'S TAXONOMY?

In the late 1940s, a group of experts in the field of education and learning set out to classify educational goals into an organized system. Because students can learn and understand information at different levels and in different ways, these educational researchers wanted to categorize the different levels of understanding from the most basic to the most complex. After years of research and study, the researchers finished their study in 1956 and published their findings in a book called *Taxonomy of educational objectives: The classification of educational goals*. The taxonomy, or classification, of those objectives is usually referred to as Bloom's Taxonomy.

Bloom's Taxonomy breaks down educational objectives into several categories that correspond to the different levels at which students can learn or understand information. The most basic level is referred to as *knowledge*. This category refers to the simple recall of facts and recognition of information. To measure a student's knowledge (as defined in Bloom's Taxonomy), teachers or tests will use questions that ask a student to do things such as list, define, name, or label. Let's look at a few examples of knowledge questions:

1. Name the capital of Texas.

2. Define the word *ecosystem*.

3. List the steps of the scientific method.

Each of the questions above requires a student to have only a basic knowledge of the subject. The GED Tests measure higher levels of thinking and understanding because the test creators know that you already have these basic skills.

The next level of Bloom's Taxonomy is *comprehension*, the subject of today's lesson. We'll examine the comprehension questions later in this lesson.

The third level of Bloom's Taxonomy is called *application*. With *application*, students apply their knowledge and demonstrate their comprehension by transferring data or principles to solve problems. Teachers and tests will use questions that ask students to solve, compute, apply, demonstrate, or use. Let's take a look at a few application questions:

1. Solve the following equation for x: $2x + 45 = 51$.

2. Demonstrate the scientific method with the biology lab experiment on page 67 of your lab manual.

Application questions will be discussed in great detail on Day 5.

The fourth level of Bloom's Taxonomy is *analysis*. With analysis, students distinguish, classify, or recognize relationships of ideas, statements, or evidence. Teachers and tests measure a student's ability to analyze by asking questions that require the student to categorize, separate, or compare and contrast. Let's take a look at a few analysis questions:

1. Compare and contrast the foreign policy of George W. Bush and Bill Clinton.

2. Separate the following list of animals into two categories, reptile or amphibian: frog, crocodile, snake, newt, iguana, toad.

Analysis questions will be discussed in great detail on Day 6.

The next level of Bloom's Taxonomy is *synthesis*. In *synthesis*, a student will combine ideas and create or originate a new idea, thought, plan, or theory. Teachers and tests measure a student's ability to synthesize by using the words develop, formulate, hypothesize, or create. Let's look at few synthesis questions:

1. Create an alternative to the Treaty of Versailles, 1919.

2. Develop a hypothesis as to the reason for global warming.

Synthesis questions will be discussed in great detail on Day 7.

The highest level of understanding within Bloom's taxonomy is *evaluation*. *Evaluation* requires a student to assess theories or presentations, discriminate between ideas, or make judgments based on reason. Teachers and tests measure a student's ability to evaluate with words such as rank, conclude, discriminate, and assess. Let's look at a few examples of evaluation questions:

1. "Evolution is the only possible explanation for modern man." Assess the validity of this statement.

2. Based on evidence presented by the Warren Commission Report, draw your own conclusion about how many shooters were involved in the assassination of President John F. Kennedy.

Along with synthesis questions, evaluation questions will be discussed in great detail on Day 7.

2. UNDERSTANDING COMPREHENSION QUESTIONS

The second level of Bloom's taxonomy is *comprehension*. Understanding and answering comprehension questions is very important to your success on the GED Tests. Comprehending an idea or concept goes beyond simply memorizing facts or definitions. Comprehension goes beyond the simple recall of information at the *knowledge* level of Bloom's Taxonomy. Comprehension involves understanding information and grasping the meaning of both words and concepts. In a test situation, comprehension can involve the location and identification of specific ideas within the context of a greater idea. A good example of this would be locating the main idea of a paragraph. Interpreting facts and inferring causes falls within the scope of comprehension as well. Comprehension can even include predicting consequences based on a series of facts or steps.

To successfully answer comprehension questions, there are a few things you should remember. First, remember the key words that will signal a comprehension question. These key words include summarize, restate, interpret, predict, distinguish, identify, recognize, and locate. If you see these words in the question, you can be sure that the question measures your comprehension skills. Second, if you determine that the question is a comprehension question based on a paragraph or paragraphs, you should look for important words, phrases, and statements within the reading passage. To find the main idea of a paragraph, look for the statement within the paragraph that sums up the rest of the text. The rest of the sentences in the paragraph will provide details that support the main idea.

3. PRACTICING COMPREHENSION QUESTIONS

Let's look at some examples of the types of questions that require comprehension and may appear on the GED Tests. Read the passages, read the questions, and circle the best answer for each question. After you answer each set, review the answer explanations.

Directions: Items 1 and 2 refer to the following paragraph.

During the 1700s, Europeans reaped many benefits of the agricultural revolution. New methods of farming increased food production on many farms. New foods added much-needed variety to the diets of many Europeans. Larger and more balanced diets bolstered the immune systems of many Europeans and helped Europeans become stronger and healthier.

1. Which of the following statements best restates the main idea of the paragraph?
    (1) During the 1700s, farming made Europeans stronger by providing labor for Europeans.
    (2) Advances in farming produced many positive results for Europeans during the 1700s.
    (3) During the 1700s, Europeans ate more than they did in other centuries.
    (4) During the 1700s, Europeans revolted against the farmers.
    (5) Farmers reaped many harvests on European farms during the 1700s.

2. Based on the information in the passage above, predict the events that followed the agricultural revolution.
    (1) Europeans became overweight because of the increase in the amount of food in their diets.
    (2) Europeans enjoyed eating much more because of the variety in their diets.
    (3) More people migrated to Europe because of the increase in available food.
    (4) The European population increased because Europeans lived longer, healthier lives.
    (5) The European population decreased even though there was more food available.

Answer Explanations

1. **The correct answer is (2).** This statement most closely restates the first sentence in the paragraph. Did you get the clue in choice (2), "many positive results," that matched one of the key words, "benefits," in the first statement of the paragraph? These kinds of clues will help you answer comprehension questions.

2. **The correct answer is (4).** It is logical to conclude that stronger, healthier people will live longer than people did before the agricultural revolution. This caused a decrease in the death rate, which contributed to the rise in population.

Directions: Item 1 refers to the following paragraph.

The Scientific Method is a series of steps one uses when performing an experiment. First, one asks a question that will be answered by the experiment. Second, one develops a hypothesis concerning the results of the experiment. Third, one conducts the experiment and observes the results. Fourth, one draws a conclusion based on the results of the experiment.

1. Which of the following statements best summarizes the paragraph?

   (1) The Scientific Method involves questioning, experimenting, and observing in order to find the answer to a question.

   (2) The Scientific Method is a long, complicated process.

   (3) The Scientific Method should be conducted only by scientists.

   (4) The Scientific Method is often inconclusive.

   (5) The Scientific Method is always thorough.

Answer Explanation

1. **The correct answer is (1).** Choice (1) restates the entire paragraph but without all the details.

Directions: Items 1 and 2 refer to the following paragraph.

(1) Basketball is a sport that requires players to have many skills. (2) Basketball players must be able to dribble the basketball with the left hand and the right hand. (3) Basketball players must be able to shoot the ball. (4) Playing defense is a must for basketball players. (5) Because players must also be able to remember plays and signals, listening is an important skill for basketball players. (6) Basketball players don't have to be tall.

1. Identify the topic sentence in the paragraph.

   (1) Sentence (1)

   (2) Sentence (2)

   (3) Sentence (4)

   (4) Sentence (5)

   (5) Sentence (6)

2. Identify the sentence that does NOT support the main idea of the paragraph.

   (1) Sentence (2)

   (2) Sentence (3)

   (3) Sentence (4)

   (4) Sentence (5)

   (5) Sentence (6)

Answer Explanations

1. **The correct answer is (1).** Sentence (1) expresses the idea that the rest of the paragraph supports.

2. **The correct answer is (5).** Sentence (6) deals with a player's height, while the topic sentence and the rest of the sentences deal with particular skills a basketball player must have.

Day 5

Answering Application and Analysis Questions

Topics for today:

1. Understanding application questions
2. Practicing application questions
3. Understanding analysis questions
4. Practicing analysis questions

1. UNDERSTANDING APPLICATION QUESTIONS

Before we begin with application questions, let's quickly review yesterday's lesson. The most basic level of learning is called knowledge. Knowledge involves memorization and recall of information and facts. The next level of learning is comprehension. Comprehension involves a thorough understanding of information and a good grasp of words, ideas, and concepts. The third level of learning and understanding is application. At the level of learning called application, one goes beyond merely comprehending information. In application, one must use both knowledge and comprehension of a subject, then apply that knowledge and comprehension to a problem or new situation. Application may also involve using required skills or knowledge to demonstrate proficiency in a particular area.

Teachers and tests often use words such as demonstrate, calculate, solve, apply, modify, or complete when they are measuring one's application skills. However, anytime a test requires the test taker to apply knowledge, the test is measuring the application skill. For example, you already have knowledge of what nouns and verbs are. You also know the role each of those parts of speech play in the English language. To measure your ability to apply that knowledge and comprehension of nouns and verbs, a test may ask you to demonstrate your skills by correctly changing or modifying a sentence's nouns and verbs in a particular way. In addition, every time you solve a math problem, you demonstrate your application skills. Everyday you solve problems and apply knowledge to new situations, which uses your application skills.

2. PRACTICING APPLICATION QUESTIONS

Let's look at some examples of the types of questions that require application and may appear on the GED Tests. Read the passages, read the questions, and circle the best answer for each question. After you answer each set, review the answer explanations.

1. Mrs. Brown has 30 students who need to purchase pencils to use on a test. Pencils cost 40 cents each at the local school supply store. Calculate the total amount of money Mrs. Brown's students will need to purchase enough pencils for the entire group.

   (1) $1.20

   (2) $12.00

   (3) $120.00

   (4) $4.30

   (5) $8.60

2. Tom needs to work between 30 and 40 hours each week to be able to afford his new car. Which of the following schedules will allow Tom to work the amount of hours he needs to afford his car?

   (1) Monday–Wednesday 9:00–4:00

   (2) Tuesday–Saturday 10:00–3:00

   (3) Tuesday, Thursday, and Saturday 11:00–9:00

   (4) Wednesday–Sunday 6:00–11:00

   (5) Monday–Saturday 8:00–12:30

Answer Explanations

1. **The correct answer is (2).** The correct calculation is 30 (students) x .40 (price per pencil) = $12.00 (total cost of pencils for Mrs. Brown's students).

2. **The correct answer is (3).** By working 10 hours (11:00–9:00) on three different days (Tuesday, Thursday, and Sunday), Tom can work 30 hours. The calculation is 3 (days) x 10 (hours) = 30 (hours needed to afford the car).

1. Choose the word that best completes the following sentence. The young girl did not want to speak in front of her class because she was _____.

   (1) ashamed

   (2) abashed

   (3) bashful

   (4) boastful

   (5) abased

2. Choose the word that best completes the following sentence. The governor said he did not get involved in the debate over the speed limit on Main Street because that was a decision to be made by the _____ government.

   (1) federal

   (2) state

   (3) constitutional

   (4) municipal

   (5) democratic

Answer Explanations

1. **The correct answer is (3).** Bashful means shy.

2. **The correct answer is (4).** A municipal government is a local, city government.

3. UNDERSTANDING ANALYSIS QUESTIONS

The fourth level of learning according to Bloom's Taxonomy is called analysis. Analysis goes beyond understanding and applying information. Analysis involves the organization of thoughts, the explanation of how parts fit together to make a whole, the identification of patterns, and the recognition and interpretation of hidden meanings. When measuring a student's ability to analyze information, teachers and tests often use words such as compare, infer, order, separate, classify, break down, or discriminate. Teachers and tests often use graphics or visuals to measure analysis skills, too. For example, a test may require you to infer something based on a picture or painting or poster.

You analyze things every day to determine hidden meanings. For example, you may consider the title of a book to determine if the title has some alternate or hidden meaning in addition to the obvious meaning. You probably also look for comparisons on a daily basis, too. Perhaps you read an article in a newspaper then read a different article on the same subject in a different newspaper; as you consider the two articles and compare the two, you are using your analysis skills. The GED Tests will measure your ability to analyze in much the same way.

4. PRACTICING ANALYSIS QUESTIONS

Let's look at some examples of the types of questions that require analysis and may appear on the GED Tests. Read the passages, read the questions, and circle the best answer for each question. After you answer each set, review the answer explanations.

Directions: Items 1 and 2 refer to the following passages.

Passage 1: "After the Great War, later referred to as World War I, the United States, Great Britain, and France joined forces and drew up terms for the defeated Germany. The terms, known as the Treaty of Versailles, blamed Germany for the war. In addition, and rightly so, Germany was forbidden from having an air force and the German army and navy were strictly limited in size. Germany was required to pay 132 billion gold marks, a sum that was not an adequate punishment in reparations, to nations it had harmed during the war."

Passage 2: "In 1919, the Big Four (Britain, France, Italy, and the United States) ganged up on Germany and instituted harsh measures against the defeated nation. The Treaty of Versailles unfairly put all the blame for the war on Germany. The treaty also crippled the German armed forces, severely limiting Germany's ability to defend herself against outside threats. Finally, the treaty required the already impoverished nation to pay an exorbitant sum of 132 billion marks in reparations."

1. Which of the following inferences can be made about the authors of the two passages above?

(1) The passages were written by the same author but at different times.

(2) The passages were written by two objective, unbiased authors.

(3) The passages were written by two authors, each of whom interpreted the Treaty of Versailles differently.

(4) World War I scholars wrote both passages.

(5) The author of each passage was careful to present factual information uncolored by his or her own opinions.

2. Which of the following appraisals can be made of the information within the passages?

(1) Passage 1 most likely appeals to those who might be sympathetic to the German situation after the war.

(2) Passage 2 most likely appeals to those who might be sympathetic to the German situation after the war.

(3) Both passages indicate that Germany was solely to blame for World War I.

(4) Both passages are presented without bias.

(5) Both passages present information based solely on research.

Answer Explanations

1. **The correct answer is (3).** A different author wrote each of the passages. Based on the difference in opinion exhibited by the text of each passage, it is clear that each author wrote from a different perspective and that each author allowed his or her bias to be revealed by the text of the passage.

2. **The correct answer is (2).** The language of the passage indicates that the author sympathized with Germany and felt that Germany was treated unfairly. The passage would definitely appeal to German sympathizers more than those who held anti-German sentiment after the war.

Directions: Item 1 is based upon the following passage.

If ever two were one, then surely we.

If ever man were loved by wife, then thee;

If ever wife was happy in a man,

Compare with me, ye women, if you can.

I prize thy love more than whole mines of gold,

Or all the riches that the East doth hold.

My love is such that rivers cannot quench,

Nor ought but love from thee, give recompense.

Thy love is such I can no way repay,

The heavens reward thee manifold, I pray.

Then while we live, in love let's so persevere

That when we live no more, we may live ever.

1. Based on the poem, which of the following is the best title for the poem?

    (1) "To My Secret Lover"

    (2) "The Anger Between Two Lovers"

    (3) "Best Friends"

    (4) "My Wife, My Best Friend"

    (5) "To My Dear and Loving Husband"

Answer Explanation

1. **The correct answer is (5).** By analyzing the lines of poetry above, you will see that the author of the poem (Anne Bradstreet) speaks in the first person about her husband. Therefore, you can infer that the only proper title is the one that mentions her husband.

Directions: Item 1 is based on the following visual.

WONDER HOW LONG THE HONEYMOON WILL LAST?

1. Which of the following is most likely the true meaning of the cartoon?

    (1) Hitler and Stalin should be partners.

    (2) Hitler and Stalin have formed a good partnership, and they should be happy with that arrangement.

    (3) Hitler and Stalin have formed a partnership whose prospects for long-term success seem uncertain.

    (4) Hitler and Stalin have formed a partnership whose honeymoon period should last a very long time.

    (5) Hitler and Stalin seem happy together, so they should form a partnership.

Answer Explanation

1. **The correct answer is (3).** Hitler and Stalin formed an alliance that surprised the rest of the world. Other countries wondered how long this unusual partnership would last. The cartoon implies that the relationship is good at the onset, but the future of the relationship is uncertain.

Day 6

Answering Synthesis and Evaluation Questions

Topics for today:

1. Understanding synthesis questions
2. Practicing synthesis questions
3. Understanding evaluation questions
4. Practicing evaluation questions

1. UNDERSTANDING SYNTHESIS QUESTIONS

Before we begin with application questions, let's briefly review Bloom's Taxonomy. The most basic level of learning is knowledge. Comprehension, the second level, uses knowledge to demonstrate a basic understanding of a concept or of information. Application, the third level, is when you apply your understanding of a concept. The next level, analysis, goes even further than application because it requires you to break down and appraise a problem and then use all the previous levels of knowledge to develop a solution to the problem.

Next in Bloom's Taxonomy is synthesis. To synthesize is to create something. Therefore, the synthesis level of learning is the level at which you combine all the previous levels of learning to create an original idea, thought, theory, proposal, or plan. In other words, to demonstrate your synthesis skills, you will need to plan, create, assemble, or organize your own thoughts and ideas. When testing this skill, a teacher or a test may use such

words as plan, propose, devise, create, construct, reconstruct, or rewrite. You probably use synthesis skills every day. If you create a proposal for your boss or if you design or construct a project, you are synthesizing. If you generate or compile a report, you are synthesizing.

On the GED, the most common place for synthesis questions to appear is on the Language Arts, Writing Test. On the Language Arts, Writing Test, you will see two types of synthesis questions. One type of synthesis question is the essay question. Remember that you will have the opportunity to write a 250-word essay on a topic that will be given to you. By formulating, developing, and writing the essay, you will be demonstrating your synthesis skills. Another type of synthesis question that you will see on the Language Arts, Writing Test will be found in the multiple-choice section of the test. Some of the multiple-choice questions will be based on a paragraph that contains errors and poorly written sentences. For some of the questions, you will need to "rewrite" a sentence. You won't actually be rewriting the sentence using pen and paper, but you will be choosing from the answer choices provided the sentence that is rewritten the best. Therefore, you will in a way be rewriting the sentence, especially if you try to answer the question in your head before you see the answer choices.

2. PRACTICING SYNTHESIS QUESTIONS

Let's look at some examples of the types of questions that require synthesis and may appear on the GED Tests. Let's look first at a few examples of questions that require you to synthesize an answer in the form of a 250-word essay. You don't have to write the essays now, but you should make yourself familiar with the types of questions you might see.

Choose one of the following topics. You have 45 minutes to draft, write, and edit an essay of about 250 words. Your essay should reflect your point of view, and you should give reasons and examples to support your position.

1. Many poorer underdeveloped countries, known as third-world countries, throughout the world have accumulated massive debt to other countries. This debt slows the economies and hinders economic progress in those countries. Should wealthier nations intervene in these situations? If so, what can the wealthier nations, such as the United States and Canada, do to help these countries? If not, why not?

2. There has been a debate concerning the authority of a government to require motorcycle riders to wear helmets, just the way car passengers must wear seatbelts. Should the government be able to make motorcycle riders wear helmets? Should motorcycle riders be able to make the decision for themselves?

3. There are as many personality traits as there are people. However, people in positions of leadership generally need some personality traits more than others do. What personality traits are most important for people in leadership positions such as office manager, administrator, personnel director, foreman, or supervisor?

Let's look at another example of the type of question that requires synthesis and may appear on the GED Tests. Read the passage, read the question, and circle the best answer for the question. After you answer the question, review the answer explanation.

Directions: Item 1 refers to the following passage.

(1) Dogs are good friends. (2) Because dogs are social animals and desire attention, many people enjoy the companionship that dogs can offer. (3) Studies have shown that dog owners often have fewer reactions to stress than do people who do not own dogs. (4) These studies have proven that dogs have a relaxing effect on people who spend time with them. (5) For that reason, therapists often take dogs to nursing homes and hospitals to cheer up the patients there.

1. Sentence (1) would be rewritten best as which of the following?
   (1) Dogs are as good as medicine.
   (2) Everyone should own a dog.
   (3) There are reasons why dogs are often called "man's best friend."
   (4) Dogs like people as much as people like dogs, so having a dog is good.
   (5) People make good companions for dogs.

Answer Explanation

1. **The correct answer is (3).** The sentences that follow sentence (1) all support the idea presented in choice (3). The other answer choices are too vague or are unrelated to the rest of the paragraph. Remember that with this question, and with similar GED questions, you are to find the best answer and not necessarily the perfect answer.

3. UNDERSTANDING EVALUATION QUESTIONS

The highest level of thinking and learning within Bloom's Taxonomy is called evaluation. Evaluation, like each of the other levels of learning already mentioned, is something that you are probably more familiar with than you think. Evaluation involves drawing on every other level of learning and then making an assessment, a judgment, a critique, or a conclusion. If you read a proposal and decide whether or not the proposal is a good idea, you are evaluating. If you listen to two arguments or two sides of an issue and make a judgment based on all your knowledge and experience, you are evaluating. Teachers and tests use words such as assess, predict, critique, evaluate, or justify when testing a student's evaluation skills.

On the GED Tests, you may see a few different evaluation questions. As with the synthesis questions, you will not necessarily write a critique, an assessment, or an evaluation using pen and paper. Instead, you will read passages and choose the best conclusion, estimation, prediction, or argument from the answer choices provided. Therefore, you will evaluate the possible answers and choose the best one.

4. PRACTICING EVALUATION QUESTIONS

Let's look at some examples of the types of questions that require evaluation and may appear on the GED Tests. Read the passages, read the questions, and circle the best answer for each question. After you answer the questions, review the answer explanations.

Directions: Item 1 refers to the following passage.

In the 1960s and 1970s, available jobs in the computer industry were relatively scarce. As computers became more affordable and more practical in the 1980s, more computer technicians and programmers were needed. During the 1990s, computers moved into nearly every facet of life. Individuals and businesses became more dependent on computers in the 1990s than ever before.

1. If this trend continues, it is safe to predict which of the following will occur in the next decade?

    (1) Computers will take over many jobs once performed by humans.

    (2) There will be an increased need for workers in the computer industry.

    (3) Computers will become more reliable, and fewer workers will be needed in the computer industry.

    (4) Eventually, the number of computers and workers in the computer industry will taper off.

    (5) Nine out of every ten individuals will go to work in the computer industry.

Answer Explanation

1. **The correct answer is (2).** By making an evaluation of the trend in the passage, you can predict that the number of computer industry jobs will increase as the number of computers increases.

Directions: Item 1 refers to the following passage.

In recent years, many people have become increasingly concerned with the amount of pollutants being released into the atmosphere. Some of these people now drive electric cars. Some of these people also refuse to use products whose manufacture occurred in factories that burn waste materials. Some even refuse to use hair spray and deodorant in aerosol cans.

1. Which of the following statements justifies or supports the concerns of the people mentioned in this passage?

   (1) Pollutants, such as those mentioned above, pose a threat to the earth's ozone layer.

   (2) Pollutants in the air make it hard for plants to grow.

   (3) Pollutants make people paranoid about the environment.

   (4) All waste products released into the atmosphere are harmful to both plants and animals.

   (5) Cars and factories are going to destroy the earth's ecosystems.

Answer Explanation

1. **The correct answer is (1).** By assessing the behavior of the people in the passage, you can determine that they are most concerned with the pollutants damaging the ozone layer. In this example, you can draw on your knowledge and comprehension of earth science, and you can analyze and assess the behavior of the people mentioned. These lower levels of learning and understanding will surely help you with your evaluation.

Day 7

Interpreting Visuals

Topics for today:

1. What is a visual?
2. Interpreting maps
3. Practicing map questions
4. Interpreting graphs
5. Practicing graph questions
6. Interpreting tables
7. Practicing table questions
8. Interpreting cartoons
9. Practicing cartoon questions

1. WHAT IS A VISUAL?

As you have already learned, most of the questions on the GED Tests will be based on reading passages. However, many of the questions will be based on visuals. Visuals are illustrations or graphics that you will need to interpret in order to answer questions. Visuals may be maps, graphs, charts, pictures, tables, political cartoons, or mathematical figures. Each of the different types of visuals conveys a particular type of information. Your task is to glean the information from the visual. If you are worried about having to identify paintings, artists, or other things that simply involve memorization, don't worry at all. Remember that the GED Tests do not test trivial or random facts and information. Just like other areas of the GED Tests, the questions dealing with visuals will test skills that you use every day. For example, the last time you took a trip, you may have used a road map to get there. The last time you read the newspaper, you probably noticed a political cartoon in the editorial section. Perhaps when you watch the news on TV, you see charts and graphs showing unemployment figures, changing gas prices, or other information.

These examples are all practical applications of the information and skills that the GED Tests will measure. We'll examine each of the types of visuals in this chapter except for mathematical visuals, which will be examined on Day 16.

2. INTERPRETING MAPS

When you encounter a map on the GED, you will probably need to answer a few questions about the map. Before you begin reading and answering the questions, look over the map carefully. You should start by reading the title of the map. Often, there is important information in the map title that will give you clues as to what information is being conveyed by the map. Next, locate the map key or legend. The map key or legend is often located off to the side or at the bottom of the map. It will explain the symbols used as well as any colors or shading used on the map. The map key or legend may also contain a map scale that indicates distances on the map.

There are a few different types of maps that you might see on the GED Tests. A political map is one that shows political boundaries, cities, states, capitals, and other political information. A topographic map shows the earth's physical features and appearance. A historical map gives information about historical times or events. A weather map shows weather patterns. A population map illustrates population density, population patterns, or the populations of cities, counties, states, regions, or countries. You can answer questions about any of these maps in basically the same way. Let's do some practice questions with maps.

---

3. PRACTICING MAP QUESTIONS

Directions: Items 1 and 2 are based on the following map

1. The majority of fishermen were located primarily in which of the following regions of the map?
    (1) Southeast
    (2) West
    (3) Northwest
    (4) North
    (5) South

2. The map most likely illustrates the primary mode of substance for which of the following groups of people?
    (1) Early American colonists
    (2) The unemployed during the Great Depression
    (3) European explorers
    (4) Early Native Americans
    (5) Early American pioneers

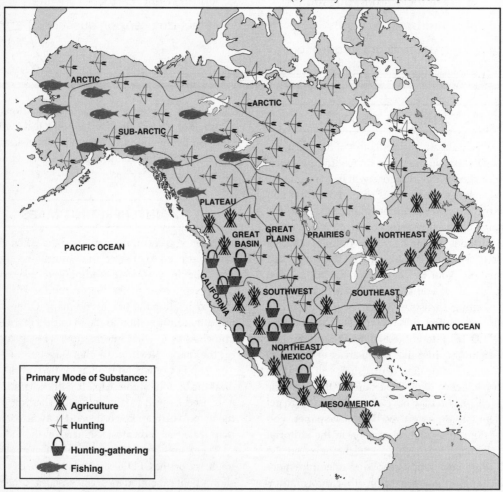

Fig. 7-2   **Circle Graph**

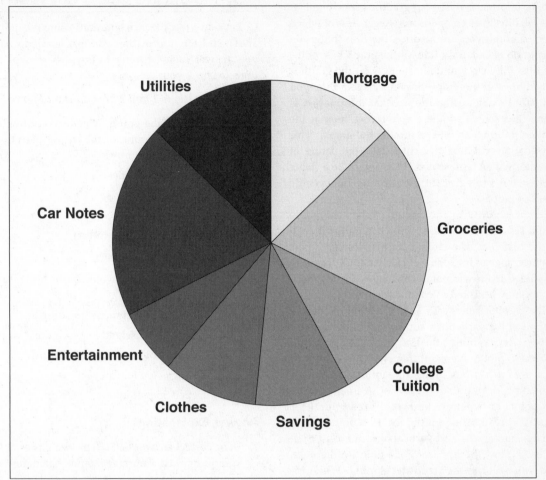

Answer Explanations

1. **The correct answer is (3).** By using the map key, you can see that fishing, represented by the fish symbol, primarily took place in the northwestern part of the continent. An elementary knowledge of geography and directions is enough here to identify the northwestern part of North America.

2. **The correct answer is (4).** A little historical knowledge and some analysis of each possible answer choice will get you the correct answer here.

4. INTERPRETING GRAPHS

Graphs are illustrations that can represent percentages, totals, and other statistical information. You may see a few different types of graphs on the GED Tests, including circle graphs, line graphs, and bar graphs. No matter which type of graph you see, there is basically one way to analyze and interpret all of them. Let's look at an example of each before we learn how to interpret the different types of graphs.

The circle graph, as illustrated in Figure 7-2, is a graph that divides a whole into parts. The line graph, as illustrated in Figure 7-3, is a graph that plots movement, increases and decreases, and other similar information. The bar graph, as shown in Figure 7-4, illustrates comparisons. Regardless of which type of graph you are reading, the first thing you should do is look for a title. If the graph has a title, the title will help you understand what the graph is illustrating. If the graph does not have a title, you will still be able to figure out what information is being represented by the graph. Next, look at the written information on and around the graph. This information will also give clues as to the nature of the information represented. Now let's take a closer look at the strategies for interpreting the specific types of graphs.

Let's begin with the circle graph. The circle graph represents a whole or 100 percent, and each of the divisions of a circle graph represents a part or percentage of the whole. On some questions you may be asked to estimate percentages of the graph, or you may be asked to compare two or more parts of the graph. This is easy as long as you remember that all of the parts must add up to 100 percent.

Next, let's examine the line graph. A line graph is used to plot movement, trends, or increases and decreases in various things like inflation, changes in income, or population growth. A line connects the points on what are known as axes (plural for axis). To read a line graph, locate a point where the horizontal axis and vertical axis intercept each other. Follow the line from one point to the next, and you will see the trend developing. When interpreting a line graph, look for patterns and sharp turns either upward or downward. As long as you follow the axes carefully, a line graph is easy to read.

Finally, let's look at the bar graph. A bar graph is used to show comparisons. Like the line graph, a bar graph will have two axes. The bars on the graph start at one axis and extend to a point that can be traced across to the other axis. The bar graph is also easy to read. On the GED Tests, bar graphs may or may not have titles, but you will be able to understand the graphs by looking carefully at all the information presented.

5. PRACTICING GRAPH QUESTIONS

Let's do a few practice questions using the graphs above and the information you just learned. After you answer each set, refer to the answer explanations to check your answers.

Directions: Items 1 and 2 are based on Figure 7-2.

1. According to the graph, which two individual expenditures account for the largest percentage of the total expenditures?

    (1) Savings and utilities

    (2) Clothes and groceries

    (3) Entertainment and clothes

    (4) Savings and college tuition

    (5) Mortgage and car notes

2. Which of the following would be the best title for this graph?

    (1) "National Government Spending"

    (2) "Monthly Household Expenditures"

    (3) "County Government Expenditures"

    (4) "Savings Plan for College"

    (5) "Deficit Spending"

Answer Explanations

1. **The correct answer is (5).** The two pieces of the graph marked "mortgage" and "car notes" together make a larger piece or percentage of the total than any other two pieces listed in the answer choices provided.

2. **The correct answer is (2).** The graph most likely represents the allocation of funds for any given household in the United States or Canada.

Fig. 7-3   **Line Graph**

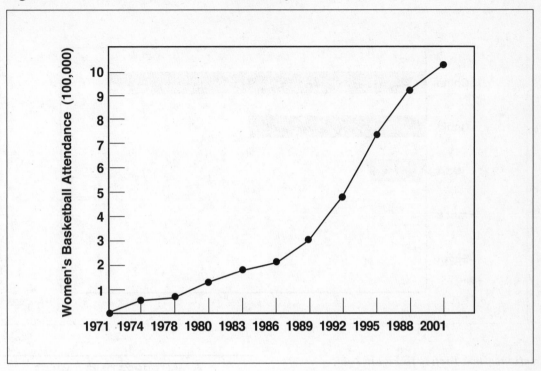

Directions: Item 1 refers to Figure 7-3.

1. According to the graph, which of the following conclusions can safely be made?

   (1) No women played basketball before 1971.

   (2) The popularity of women's basketball made major strides between 1977 and 1980.

   (3) The popularity of women's basketball made major strides between 1992 and 1995.

   (4) Women's basketball was just as popular in 1989 as in 1979.

   (5) Men's basketball has always been more popular than women's basketball.

Answer Explanation

1. **The correct answer is (3).** Between 1992 and 1995, women's basketball attendance increased sharply and began an upward trend. Therefore, it is safe to say that attendance increased because of an increase in popularity between 1992 and 1995.

Fig. 7-4 **Bar Graph**

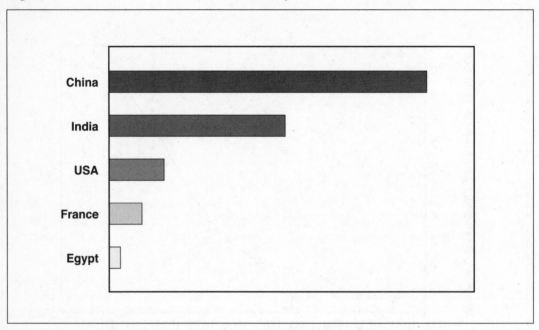

Directions: Item 1 refers to Figure 7-4.

1. Which of the following does the graph most likely represent?

   (1) Population of each country

   (2) Years of existence as a country

   (3) Annual per capita income of each country

   (4) Number of Wonders of the World within each country

   (5) Number of registered voters in each country

Answer Explanation

1. **The correct answer is (1).** A basic knowledge of the world's population will help you see that China and India are two of the most populous countries in the world, and these countries have the longest bars in this graph. Even without two axes, this graph clearly represents population.

6. INTERPRETING TABLES

Some of the visuals on the GED Tests will be tables. Questions based on a table will generally measure your ability to read and understand the table as well as your ability to use the information in the table. To interpret a table, first read the title of the table. Next, read the titles of the rows and columns in the table. Where the rows and columns intersect, there will be numbers or figures. These numbers and figures represent the relationship between the row and column. Before you start surveying the figures in the table, read the question so you'll have an idea of what information you are looking for in the table. Now you are ready to start answering the questions based on the table.

7. PRACTICING TABLE QUESTIONS

Let's do a practice question based on a table. After you answer the question, refer to the answer explanation for the correct answer.

Fig. 7-5   **Airline Flight Reliability, 1960-2000**

Year	On Time Passenger Flights	On Time Cargo Flights	Cancelled Passenger Flights	Cancelled Cargo Flights
1960	96.7%	97.5%	1.2%	.9%
1970	91.3%	95.4%	2.6%	1.7%
1980	90.4%	93.0%	4.0%	2.8%
1990	83.2%	87.7%	6.1%	3.3%
2000	80.6%	86.2%	6.4%	5.5%

Directions: Item 1 is based on Figure 7-5.

1. Which of the following conclusions can be made safely based on the table?

   (1) Technology has not really helped flights any since 1960.

   (2) The safest year to fly was 1960.

   (3) The time between 1980 and 1990 saw the greatest increase in challenges to airline passenger flight reliability.

   (4) Flights were safer, more comfortable, and less crowded in 1980 than in 1990.

   (5) Cargo flights have never been as reliable as passenger flights since 1960.

Answer Explanation

1. **The correct answer is (3).** Based on the table, the reliability saw the greatest decrease between 1980 and 1990. This means that for some reasons not given in the table, there were factors that affected the reliability between 1980 and 1990.

8. INTERPRETING CARTOONS

If you have read the editorial section of the newspaper or in a magazine lately, you probably noticed a political cartoon. A political cartoon is a cartoon that expresses the artist's opinion about a particular issue. Often the artist will use satire, or witty sarcasm, to make his or her point. In other words, the cartoon may be making fun of someone or something to make a point. You will probably see a political cartoon or two on the GED Tests. Interpreting cartoons is not difficult if you know what to look for. First, read the caption and/or title. This will give you some clue about the meaning of the cartoon. Remember, because the artist may be using satire, the words in the title or caption may have multiple meanings. Next, try to find recognizable people, places, or things in the cartoon. This will also give a clue about the meaning of the cartoon. Finally, try to determine what is happening in the cartoon. As you do this, keep in mind the title or caption. Once you put all the clues together, you will have interpreted the cartoon.

9. PRACTICING CARTOON QUESTIONS

Let's put all three steps together and practice on the cartoon below. After you have examined the cartoon and answered the question, see the answer explanation for the correct answer.

Directions: Item 1 refers to the following cartoon.

1. What conclusion can be drawn based on the cartoon above?

   (1) The U.S. was in a race with the Soviet Union to help rebuild Western Europe.

   (2) The U.S. felt as though communism might have spread chaos in Western Europe if Congress did not offer assistance to Western European nations.

   (3) Communists felt as though the U.S. Congress was being reckless with its foreign policy.

   (4) Western Europe needed assistance so badly that it would open its doors to democracy and communism as long as those nations received assistance.

   (5) The U.S. and the Soviets were racing to get out of Eastern Europe, and Western Europe was the only safe place to go.

Answer Explanation

1. **The correct answer is (2).** The United States wanted to help rebuild Western European nations so it would have influence over the Western European nations and not the Soviets. Notice that the car labeled "Doctor U.S. Congress" appears to be racing the bird labeled "communism," which is carrying "chaos." "Communism" represents the threat of the former Soviet Union. Obviously, the United States would not want its former enemy, the Soviet Union, to have any influence on other parts of the world.

Day 8

Understanding Passages of Literature and Related Passages

Topics for today:

1. Understanding Fiction
2. Practicing with Fiction
3. Understanding Drama
4. Practicing with Drama
5. Understanding Poetry
6. Practicing with Poetry
7. Understanding Nonfiction and Commentary
8. Practicing with Nonfiction and Commentary

1. UNDERSTANDING FICTION

Some of the reading passages you will see on the GED will be passages of fiction. Fiction simply means that a written work is based on someone's imagination. In other words, the story, characters, and other elements of the fiction work are made up by the author. Even stories based on real people or real situations can be fiction. Most fiction is either a short story or a novel, a longer work of fiction. To understand fiction, there are several terms that you must understand. Let's look at some of the more common terms used when talking about works of fiction.

The first two important terms you need to understand when dealing with fiction are **first person** and **third person**. These terms are used to describe the point of view from which a work of fiction is written; most fiction is expressed in either first or third person. If the work is written in first person, the author of the fiction uses a narrator, or storyteller, to tell the story from his or her point of view. That narrator speaks in terms of "I," "me," or "my" when telling the story, so the story is told from the narrator's perspective as seen through the narrator's eyes. When reading a first person work of fiction, the reader is limited by the narrator's limited knowledge; the reader knows only what the narrator sees. On the other hand, a third-person story is told from the perspective of a narrator who knows and reveals everything to the reader. In a third-person work of fiction, the narrator does not speak in terms of "I" but rather in terms of "he," "she," and "they." A work of fiction written in third person allows the reader glimpses of all the characters' actions and feelings.

The story within a work of fiction is referred to as the **plot**. The events that make up the plot of a work of fiction can be put together in a few different ways. The way the events unfold within a story is called the **sequence**. Events can flow chronologically and in sequence, or events can be revealed out of order or out of sequence. The figures involved in the plot are known as **characters**. The main characters are those around whom the plot revolves. Minor characters are incidental characters that become involved in the plot to some extent through the course of the story. The place, time, and conditions in which the plot unfolds is referred to as the **setting**. The way the narrator tells the story and influences the feelings of the reader is known as the **tone,** and the overall feeling or atmosphere of the story is called the **mood**.

2. PRACTICING WITH FICTION

Let's look at a few examples of questions that are based on a work of fiction. After you answer the questions, read the answer explanations for the correct answers.

Directions: Items 1 and 2 refer to the following passage.

During the whole of a dull, dark, and soundless day in the autumn of the year, when the clouds hung oppressively low in the heavens, I had been passing alone, on horseback, through a singularly dreary tract of country; and at length found myself, as the shades of the evening drew on, within view of the melancholy House of Usher. I know not how it was—but, with the first glimpse of the building, a sense of insufferable gloom pervaded my spirit. I say insufferable; for the feeling was unrelieved by any of that half-pleasurable, because poetic, sentiment, with which the mind usually receives even the sternest natural images of the desolate or terrible. I looked upon the scene before me—upon the mere house, and the simple landscape features of the domain—upon the bleak walls—upon the vacant eye-like windows—upon a few rank sedges—and upon a few white trunks of decayed trees—with an utter depression of soul which I can compare to no earthly sensation more properly than to the after-dream of the reveler upon opium—the bitter lapse into everyday life—the hideous dropping off of the veil. There was an iciness, a sinking, a sickening of the heart—an unredeemed dreariness of thought which no goading of the imagination could torture into aught of the sublime. What was it—I paused to think—what was it that so unnerved me in the contemplation of the House of Usher? It was a mystery all insoluble; nor could I grapple with the shadowy fancies that crowded upon me as I pondered. I was forced to fall back upon the unsatisfactory conclusion, that while, beyond doubt, there are combinations of very simple natural objects which have the power of thus affecting us, still the analysis of this power lies among considerations beyond our depth. It was possible, I reflected, that a mere different arrangement of the particulars of the scene, of the details of the picture, would be sufficient to modify, or perhaps to annihilate its capacity for sorrowful impression; and, acting upon this idea, I reined my horse to the precipitous brink of a black and lurid tarn that lay in unruffled luster by the dwelling, and gazed down—but with a shudder even more thrilling than before—upon the remodeled and inverted images of the gray sedge, and the ghastly tree-stems, and the vacant and eye-like windows.

from *The Fall of the House of Usher*
by Edgar Allan Poe

1. Which of the following phrases best describes the setting of the passage?

    (1) A bright, sunny day in the city

    (2) A bright, sunny day somewhere in the countryside

    (3) A dreary day in the city

    (4) A dreary day somewhere in the countryside

    (5) A cold, snowy day near a river

2. Which term best describes the mood of the passage?

    (1) Dark

    (2) Optimistic

    (3) Evil

    (4) Heavenly

    (5) Jocular

Answer Explanations

1. **The correct answer is (4).** The first sentence of the passage gives clues about the setting of the story.

2. **The correct answer (1).** The use of the eerie, gloomy language throughout the passage makes the mood dark.

3. UNDERSTANDING DRAMA

Although drama is written for actors and actresses to perform on a stage, many people read drama for entertainment just as they would read fiction. At first glance, a page of drama looks much different than a page of fiction, but if you remember a few things you should have no trouble reading and understanding drama. First, you will see that works of drama are divided into **acts** and **scenes** instead of chapters. At the beginning of each act or scene, the playwright, or author of the drama, will briefly describe the setting. Although that description is intended for the director and actors, readers of drama can infer much information about the drama based on the description at the beginning of the acts and scenes. Second, you will notice that the text of the drama is in the form of **dialogue**, or the words spoken by the actors and actresses. The lines of dialogue will follow the name of the character who speaks the lines on stage. The challenge of a playwright is to write the character's dialogue in such a way that the dialogue tells the audience, or reader in your case, exactly what the character is thinking and feeling. If a character needs to perform a certain action on stage to convey information to the audience, the playwright will write **stage directions** either before or after the character's dialogue. By reading the dialogue and stage directions, you can follow the actions, thoughts, and feelings of the characters. It is important to read every line in a work of drama so that you can make all the necessary inferences. It is also important for you to use your imagination when reading drama since you will not be reading paragraphs of descriptive sentences as in a work of fiction.

4. PRACTICING WITH DRAMA

Let's look at an example of a question that is based on a work of drama. After you answer the questions, read the answer explanation for the correct answer.

Directions: Item 1 is based on the following passage, an excerpt from William Shakespeare's **Romeo and Juliet.**

Lady Capulet: Marry, that 'marry' is the very theme I came to talk of. Tell me, daughter Juliet, How stands your disposition to be married?

Juliet: It is an honour that I dream not of.

Nurse: An honour! were not I thine only nurse, I would say thou hadst suck'd wisdom from thy teat.

Lady Capulet: Well, think of marriage now; younger than you, Here in Verona, ladies of esteem, Are made already mothers: by my count, I was your mother much upon these years That you are now a maid. Thus then in brief: The valiant Paris seeks you for his love.

Nurse: A man, young lady! lady, such a man As all the world—why, he's a man of wax.

Lady Capulet: Verona's summer hath not such a flower.

Nurse: Nay, he's a flower; in faith, a very flower.

Lady Capulet: What say you? can you love the gentleman? This night you shall behold him at our feast; Read o'er the volume of young Paris' face, And find delight writ there with beauty's pen; Examine every married lineament, And see how one another lends content And what obscured in this fair volume lies Find written in the margent of his eyes. This precious book of love, this unbound lover, To beautify him, only lacks a cover: The fish lives in the sea, and 'tis much pride For fair without the fair within to hide: That book in many's eyes doth share the glory, That in gold clasps locks in the golden story; So shall you share all that he doth possess, By having him, making yourself no less.

Nurse: No less! nay, bigger; women grow by men.

Lady Capulet: Speak briefly, can you like of Paris' love?

Juliet: I'll look to like, if looking liking move: But no more deep will I endart mine eye Than your consent gives strength to make it fly.

[Enter a Servant]

1. What are Lady Capulet and the Nurse trying to convince Juliet to do in the passage?

    (1) Read a beautiful, unbound book

    (2) Smell a flower

    (3) Consider marrying Paris

    (4) Move to the city of Paris

    (5) Go fishing in the sea

Answer Explanation

1. **The correct answer is (3).** The two older women are trying to encourage Juliet to look at Paris and see if she might consider marrying him.

---

5. UNDERSTANDING POETRY

For many people, the idea of reading and understanding poetry seems like a daunting task. However, just like reading and understanding other works of literature, reading and understanding poetry simply involves understanding a few basic concepts and vocabulary words. The most important thing to understand about poetry is its purpose. Poetry usually creates an image or expresses the ideas and feelings of the poet or author. Occasionally, though, poetry tells a story. Either way, poets use a number of literary tools to express their ideas. Let's look at some of the figurative language that poets often use to create poems.

Rather than rely on everyday language to create poems, poets often use figurative language to make their poetry more creative and imaginative. Two good examples of such figurative language are **similes** and **metaphors**. A simile is a word that makes a comparison using either the word *like* or *as*. Here are a few examples of similes:

She was quiet *as* a mouse, but he roared *like* a ferocious lion.

A metaphor, on the other hand, makes a comparison by identifying two seemingly different words. Here is an example of a metaphor:

War *is* hell.

Poets also use a technique called **personification** to create an image and make their writing more interesting. Personification is giving humanlike characteristics or qualities to an object. Here is an example of personification:

The wind sang a beautiful lullaby as it gently blew through the orchard.

To create a rhythm or a unique sound for a poem, a poet may use **alliteration**. Alliteration is the use of several words beginning with the same letter in order to give a line of poetry an almost-musical quality. Here's an example of alliteration:

The fluttering butterfly floated and frolicked in the field of flowers.

Some poets use a tool called **onomatopoeia** to create a different kind of musical effect for their poems. With onomatopoeia, a poet tries to articulate a particular sound through the use of words; the sounds may be the sound of a bell, the sound of raindrops, the sound of a cannon, or some other sound. Here's an example of onomatopoeia:

Drip drop drip drop drip drop went the leaky faucet.

When you are reading poetry, keep in mind that poets use all of these tools to create images and express feelings in a way that isn't done as often in works of fiction or nonfiction.

Another important part of understanding poetry is knowing how to read poetry. Some poetry is written so that some of the lines rhyme, while other poetry, called free verse, is written so that the lines do not rhyme. Regardless of whether or not the poetry rhymes, there are a few things to remember when reading a poem. As you read, let the lines flow from one to the next, except at punctuation marks. Also, think about the poem as a whole, and do not get bogged down trying to analyze every line. If you keep all these points in mind, you should have little difficulty reading and understanding poetry.

6. PRACTICING WITH POETRY

Let's look at a few examples of questions that are based on a work of poetry. After you answer the questions, read the answer explanations for the correct answers.

Directions: Items 1 and 2 refer to the following passage from Samuel Taylor Coleridge's "The Rime of the Ancient Mariner."

Down dropped the breeze, the sails dropped down,
Twas sad as sad could be;
And we did speak only to break
The silence of the sea!
All in a hot and copper sky,
The bloody Sun, at noon,
Right up above the mist did stand,
No bigger than the Moon.
Day after day, day after day,
We stuck, nor breath nor motion;
As idle as a painted ship
Upon a painted ocean.
Water, water, everywhere,
And all the boards did shrink;
Water, water, everywhere,
Nor any drop to drink.

1. Which of the following scenarios is this passage most likely describing?

    (1) Travelers lost in the desert

    (2) Sailors caught in a fierce storm

    (3) Soldiers resting after a battle

    (4) Astronauts in space

    (5) Sailors lost at sea

2. Which of the following lines uses a simile to make a comparison?

    (1) Upon a painted ocean

    (2) The bloody sun

    (3) Twas sad as sad could be

    (4) As idle as a painted ship

    (5) No bigger than the moon

Answer Explanations

1. **The correct answer is (5).** This passage is about the despair of sailors whose ship is lost at sea.

2. **The correct answer is (4).** This line uses *as* to make a comparison between the sailors' ship and a ship in a painting.

7. UNDERSTANDING NONFICTION AND COMMENTARY

Unlike fiction, poetry, and drama, works of nonfiction are any literary works that claim to be true. A nonfiction work might be an essay or a narrative. Understanding a nonfiction work may be much easier for you than understanding fiction, because authors use figurative language less frequently in nonfiction. The key to understanding a work of nonfiction is this: read the passage carefully and look for the main idea of each paragraph. The main idea is often located in the first sentence of the paragraph. Also, the first paragraph of the passage often indicates the main idea of the entire passage. In some cases, though, the main idea of a paragraph is found in the last sentence of the paragraph.

One particular kind of nonfiction that you will see on the GED is called commentary. In a commentary, the author offers a critique or evaluation of a book, a play, another literary work, or perhaps even a piece of art or music. That a commentary is considered nonfiction does not necessarily make the passage true. A commentary is simply a way that an author expresses his or her opinion. Sometimes an author will not clearly state his or her opinion but will use language, phrases, and statements that offer clues about his or her opinion. Your task will be to determine the author's opinion or point of view based on the language used in the commentary. A good clue as to the author's opinion is the **tone** of the language. The tone is a reflection of the author's thoughts and feelings. A commentary may have a positive tone or it may have a negative tone. The language the author uses often will indicate the tone of the commentary.

8. Practicing with Nonfiction and Commentary

Let's look at an example of a question that is based on a work of nonfiction. After you answer the question, read the answer explanation for the correct answer.

Directions: Item 1 refers to the following excerpt from an essay by Michel Montaigne.

It is not enough to fortify his soul: you are also to make his sinews strong; for the soul will be oppressed if not assisted by the members, and would have too hard a task to discharge two offices alone. I know very well, to my cost, how much mine groans under the burden, from being accommodated with a body so tender and indisposed, as eternally leans and presses upon her; and often in my reading perceive that our masters, in their writings, make examples pass for magnanimity and fortitude of mind, which really are rather toughness of skin and hardness of bones; for I have seen men, women, and children, naturally born of so hard and insensible a constitution of body, that a sound cudgeling has been less to them than a flirt with a finger would have been to me, and that would neither cry out, wince, nor shrink, for a good swinging beating; and when wrestlers counterfeit the philosophers in patience, 'tis rather strength of nerves than stoutness of heart.

1. The subject of the essay is most likely which of the following?
   (1) Physical education of a child in addition to intellectual education
   (2) Physical abuse of a child
   (3) Making philosophers strong
   (4) The amazing strength of the author
   (5) The pathetic weakness of the author

Answer Explanation

1. **The correct answer is (1).** The author argues that in addition to fortifying a child's soul, an adult should also consider working to improve a child's physical condition.

Let's look at an example of a question that is based on a commentary. After you answer the question, read the answer explanation for the correct answer.

Directions: Item 1 is based on the following passage, which is a commentary by C. S. Barber.

There are nine installments in the succession of Christian books known as the "Left Behind" series. Tim LaHaye and Jerry B. Jenkins, whose storytelling is based on their interpretation of the book of Revelations, write the series. Through the lives of a few people, the authors explore life at the time of the Rapture, or return of Christ. Chaos abounds and few understand why so many people have vanished. As the characters who were left behind come to understand, and eventually accept, the reality of what has happened, they join forces to prepare for the years of adversity to come. We read as they prepare to fight the ultimate battle between good and evil. Each new addition to the series brings the heroes closer to the end of the Tribulation and ultimately to a reunion with Christ.

LaHaye and Jenkins bring Revelations into reality and clearly describe how they envision life after the Rapture. Whether prophecy or just good, old-fashioned story-telling, each story is undoubtedly captivating. The Left Behind series is an anomaly in Christian literature. With each book outselling the last, LaHaye and Jenkins are as popular as any other authors on the market. With popularity like this, book ten, expected in Summer of 2002, will undoubtedly be a best-seller.

1. Which of the following statements most accurately reflects the attitude of the author based on the tone of the commentary?

    (1) The "Left Behind" series of books is merely a trend that will soon pass.

    (2) The "Left Behind" series of books is only popular in a certain market.

    (3) The "Left Behind" series of books contains great characters and good stories.

    (4) The "Left Behind" series of books has little appeal.

    (5) The "Left Behind" series of books has good stories but poor writing.

Answer Explanation

1. **The correct answer is (3).** The author's tone is very positive and complimentary throughout the commentary.

Day 9

Understanding Adult-Context Documents and Practical Documents

Topics for today:

1. What are Adult-Context Documents and Practical Documents?
2. Adult-Context Documents on the Language Arts, Writing Test
3. Adult-Context Documents on the Language Arts, Reading Test
4. Practical Documents on the Social Studies Test

1. WHAT ARE ADULT-CONTEXT DOCUMENTS AND PRACTICAL DOCUMENTS?

Because the GED Tests are designed to measure skills that you will need and use in the workplace, the GED Tests will include several types of documents that you are sure to encounter once you enter the business world. If you are already in the workforce, you have surely seen several of these kinds of documents. Whether you will be an employee or an employer, you will need to be familiar with several types of documents that the GED refers to as Adult-Context Documents and Practical Documents. The documents may include, but are not limited to, memos, business letters, reports, job applications, excerpts from employee handbooks, excerpts from training manuals, and institutional mission statements. Other informational documents, or reading passages, that you may see may include, but are not limited to, tax forms and voter's guides.

All of these documents will not necessarily be used on the same test section. Likewise, you may not encounter all of these documents during your entire GED test-taking experience. However, it is important that you become familiar with each so that you are ready for anything you may see on the GED Tests.

2. ADULT-CONTEXT DOCUMENTS ON THE LANGUAGE ARTS, WRITING TEST

The Adult-Context Documents on the Language Arts, Writing test will include business communications such as letters, memos, emails, reports, and job applications. These documents will appear on the multiple-choice section of the Language Arts, Writing Test and not on the essay section. Because they appear on the multiple-choice section, these documents will contain errors that you will need to correct. The errors within these documents may include poor sentence structure, incorrect word usage, or incorrectly used homonyms, possessives, and contractions. Therefore, when you read through these documents, look for errors that might affect the meaning of the sentences or the meaning of the document. Also, look for errors that weaken the writing. Finally, look for errors that simply appear to be careless mistakes. These are all the kinds of errors that an employer would want you to be able to avoid if you were to write a similar document or to find if you were to read a similar document. Let's do a few practice questions based on some Adult-Context Documents. After you answer each set, refer to the answer explanation for the correct answers.

Directions: Items 1 and 2 refer to the following document.

Interoffice Memo Regarding Casual Fridays:

(1) Beginning on Friday, January 17, 2002, all employee's of the Acme Accounting Firm will be permitted to dress casually each Friday. (2) These "casual dress days" will henceforth be referred to as Casual Fridays. (3) The company dress code requiring men to wear suits and women to wear business suits will not apply to men and women on Fridays. (4) Blue jeans will be considered appropriate attire. (5) T-shirts and/or shorts will be considered inappropriate. (6) Management encourages employees to enjoy the freedom of Casual Fridays while still dressing in good taste.

1. Beginning on Friday, January 17, 2002, all employee's of the Acme Accounting Firm will be permitted to dress casually each Friday.

   What correction should be made?

   (1) Remove <u>be permitted to</u>
   (2) Change <u>employee's</u> to <u>employees</u>
   (3) Change <u>each</u> to <u>on every</u>
   (4) Change <u>be</u> to <u>bee</u>
   (5) No correction is necessary

2. The company dress code requiring men to wear suits and women to wear business suits will not apply to men and women on Fridays.

   What correction should be made?

   (1) Change <u>wear</u> to <u>where</u>
   (2) Change <u>suits</u> and <u>suits</u> to <u>suit's</u> and <u>suit's</u>
   (3) Change <u>Friday</u> to <u>Friday's</u>
   (4) Remove <u>to men and women</u>
   (5) No correction is necessary

Answer Explanation

1. **The correct answer is (2).** The word <u>employees</u> should be plural and not possessive.

2. **The correct answer is (4).** The phrase <u>to men and women</u> weakens the writing and is unnecessary.

Directions: Items 1 and 2 refer to the following document.

Excerpt from letter to Smith County employees concerning the Smith County Drug and Alcohol Abuse Policy

(1) Employees are prohibited from the use, sale, dispensing, distribution, possession, or manufacture of illegal drugs, narcotics, inhalants, alcoholic beverages, drug paraphernalia, or other controlled substances on county premises or work cites. (2) Employees are prohibitive from being under the influence of illegal drugs, narcotics, inhalants, alcoholic beverages, or other controlled substances during work hours.

1. Employees are prohibited from the use, sale, dispensing, distribution, possession, or manufacture of illegal drugs, narcotics, inhalants, alcoholic beverages, drug paraphernalia, or other controlled substances on county premises or work sites.

   What correction can be made?

   (1) Change <u>Employees</u> to <u>Employee's</u>
   (2) Change <u>prohibited</u> to <u>exhibited</u>
   (3) Change <u>manufacture</u> to <u>manufactured</u>
   (4) Change <u>cites</u> to <u>sites</u>
   (5) No correction is necessary

2. Employees are prohibitive from being under the influence of illegal drugs, narcotics, inhalants, alcoholic beverages, or other controlled substances during work hours.

   What correction can be made?

   (1) Change <u>prohibitive</u> to <u>prohibited</u>
   (2) Change <u>illegal</u> to <u>legal</u>
   (3) Remove <u>from</u>
   (4) Change <u>hours</u> to <u>ours</u>
   (5) No correction is necessary

Answer Explanations

1. **The correct answer is (4).** "Cites" is the wrong word to use here; the correct word is "sites."

2. **The correct answer is (1).** "Prohibitive" is the wrong word to use here; the correct word is "prohibited."

3. ADULT-CONTEXT DOCUMENTS ON THE LANGUAGE ARTS, READING TEST

The Adult-Context Documents on the Language Arts, Reading Test differ slightly from those you just learned about. On the Language Arts, Reading Test, you will read documents, including excerpts from employee handbooks, training manuals, or institutional mission statements. These documents often will be 12–18 sentences in length or 200–300 words in length. Instead of looking for errors within the documents, you will be using your comprehension, application, analysis, and synthesis skills to answer questions about the documents. As you read the documents, you should look for things like the main idea of the document, the point of view of the author, and the intended audience. These bits of information will help you answer any questions about the documents. Let's do a few practice questions based on some Adult-Context Documents within the scope of the Language Arts, Reading Test. After you answer each set, refer to the answer explanation for the correct answers.

Directions: Items 1 and 2 are based on the following document.

> Employees should have no expectation of privacy regarding their use of the Internet. All records created by Internet use, including path records, are subject to inspection and audit by management, or its representatives, at any time, with or without notice. Use of the county's Internet system by an employee indicates that the employee understands that the county has a right to inspect and audit all Internet use; and consents to any inspections following proper procedures and protocols as determined by commissioners court.

In general, the Internet should be used only for official county business; however, brief and occasional surfing and browsing for non-business reasons is acceptable. Personal use of the Internet should not impede the conduct of county business; only incidental amounts of employee time, time periods comparable to reasonable coffee breaks during the day, should be to attend to personal matters. Excess personal use of the Internet may result in appropriate disciplinary action. Personal use of the Internet should not cause the county to incur a direct cost in addition to the general overhead of the Internet system. Consequently, employees should not store or print personal Internet material.

1. Which of the following is a summary of the first paragraph?
   (1) County employees can only use the county Internet system in private.
   (2) County employees can use the county Internet system for audits and inspections.
   (3) County employees should be aware that the county can monitor employees' use of the county Internet system at any time.
   (4) County employees must consent to Internet inspections.
   (5) Commissioners courts must audit all county employees.

2. Based on the second paragraph, county employees are expected to do which of the following?
   (1) Spend no more than a few minutes each day using the Internet for personal reasons
   (2) Print and save no more than a reasonable amount of Internet information
   (3) Incur only minimal costs above overhead for the county
   (4) Spend no time each day using the Internet for personal reasons
   (5) Use the county Internet system only while on coffee breaks

Answer Explanations

1. **The correct answer is (3).** The first line of the paragraph indicates that employees should not expect to have privacy concerning the use of the county Internet system.

2. **The correct answer is (1).** The policy says that employees should spend no more time using the Internet for personal reasons than they would for a reasonable coffee break, a break that would only be a few minutes.

Directions: Item 1 refers to the following document.

The Women's Service Association is an organization of over 500 women in the community committed to promoting voluntarism, developing the potential of women, and improving our community through effective action and leadership of trained volunteers. During its 75-year history, the Women's Service Association has initiated hundreds of community improvement projects through partnerships with local agencies, churches, and educational institutions. The Women's Service Association's commitment to the quality of life in Washington County is demonstrated by our educational and community outreach projects. Each is designed to improve the physical, intellectual, and emotional development of children and adolescents.

1. According to the mission statement above, it can be concluded safely that which of the following can be attributed to the Women's Service Organization?

   (1) Construction of a gazebo at a retirement home

   (2) Fundraising for a political candidate

   (3) Construction of an inner-city children's library

   (4) Sponsorship of a men-only educational seminar

   (5) Sponsorship of a soup kitchen for the unemployed

Answer Explanation

1. **The correct answer is (3).** While all the answer choices are worthy service projects, an inner-city children's library is the only project that complies with the last sentence of the mission statement.

4. PRACTICAL DOCUMENTS ON THE SOCIAL STUDIES TEST

The real-world documents used on the Social Studies section of the GED are referred to as Practical Documents. Practical Documents are social studies related documents that you will encounter very soon if you haven't already. The most common practical documents that you are likely to see on the GED Social Studies Test are tax forms and voter's guides. The questions based on these documents will measure your ability to analyze the documents for basic economic and political principles. When you read Practical Documents, look first for the main idea or for the instructions in the document. Next, consider the economic or political principles represented by the document. For example, if an excerpt from a voter's guide explains how to choose a candidate for a particular office from one party or another, you have just read a document that is related to the two-party political system. Let's do a few practice questions based on a Practical Document similar to what you might see on the Social Studies Test. After you answer the questions, refer to the answer explanation for the correct answers.

Directions: Item 1 refers to the document below.

To obtain a civilian absentee ballot, apply by mail that is delivered to the county clerk at least seven days before the election, or apply in person by 3:00 p.m. the day before the election. The application should include the date of the election, your home address including municipality, address to where ballot should be sent, and reason for request. Sign the application with the same signature used at the polls. After approval of the application, a ballot and instructions will be mailed to you. If application is made in person within the seven-day period before the election, the ballot will be given to you at that time. Absentee ballots must reach the County Board of Elections before the close of polls on election day. If you have applied for an absentee ballot, you MAY NOT VOTE at your polling place for that election, regardless of whether or not you completed the absentee ballot. If ill or incapacitated, you may send written authorization with a family member or registered voter within your county to obtain your ballot and return it to the county clerk's office within the above time frame. To obtain a military absentee ballot, the voter, a relative, or friend may apply to your county clerk or municipal clerk. Applications can also be requested from the proper military personnel.

Civilian absentee ballots are available to registered voters who cannot vote in person for the following reasons: expect to be absent from the state on election day, illness or disability, observance of a religious holiday, residing at an educational institution, or hours and nature of employment. Military absentee ballots are available to registered or unregistered citizens of voting age who are in military service or the spouses or dependents of those in military, service civilians attached to the armed forces and their spouses or dependents, or patients in veterans hospitals.

1. Which of the following would be a legitimate reason to vote via absentee ballot?

    (1) A fear of voting booths

    (2) On active military duty in Afghanistan

    (3) A desire to vote before the actual election

    (4) A desire to vote after the actual election

    (5) Lack of transportation to the polls

2. Absentee ballots are used in the United States for which of the following reasons?

    (1) To prevent noncitizens from voting

    (2) To avoid paying poll taxes

    (3) To avoid age discrimination

    (4) To allow any political party to vote

    (5) To allow all citizens an opportunity to vote, even if a citizen cannot be at the polls on election day

Answer Explanations

1. **The correct answer is (2).** Those men and women in military service away from their homes can use absentee ballots.

2. **The correct answer is (5).** Absentee ballots help ensure the success of the democratic process by giving as many citizens as possible the opportunity to participate in the electoral process.

Day 10

Preparing for Language Arts, Writing

Topics for today:

1. Introduction to the Language Arts, Writing Test
2. Part I—The Multiple-Choice Section
3. Part II—The Essay Section
4. Parts of Speech
5. Sentence Structure
6. Paragraphs
7. Practicing Language Arts, Writing Questions

1. INTRODUCTION TO THE LANGUAGE ARTS, WRITING TEST

The Language Arts, Writing Test measures two skills. First, with Part I or the multiple-choice section, the Language Arts, Writing Test will measure your ability to read a document and find errors within the text of the document. Second, with Part II or the essay section, the Language Arts, Writing Test will measure your ability to write. On the essay, you will be expected to employ proper grammar and word usage as well as good sentence and paragraph organization. Even though there are two parts, the two parts will be reported as a single score. Therefore, in order to receive credit for the Language Arts, Writing Test, you must successfully complete both parts of the test. Let's take a closer look at each of the two parts of the test.

2. PART I—THE MULTIPLE-CHOICE SECTION

Part I of the Language Arts, Writing Test consists of 50 multiple-choice questions. Each question will have five possible answer choices numbered 1–5. You will have 75 minutes to complete this part of the test. The multiple-choice questions will be based on a number of different reading passages called information documents. Each document will have several sentences that contain errors of some kind. Following each document will be several questions that refer to the document. This part of the test will measure your ability to locate the errors within the text and choose the best possible corrections or revisions for the errors. There may be some sentences that have no errors, and you will need to choose the answer choice that indicates no correction is necessary.

The documents will be up to approximately 200–300 words in length and may contain as many as 12–18 sentences. While the topics of the documents are not necessarily important, you may be interested in knowing what kinds of documents you will be reading. Some of the documents may be excerpts from stories or articles. Others may include business communications in the form of memos, e-mails, or letters. Still other documents will be how-to texts that explain how to plan a vacation or how to buy or sell a car. Regardless of the type of document you read, you will be looking for the same kinds of errors within the text. The multiple-choice section will include questions that will require revision because of errors within the sentence. Some of these errors include misuse of homonyms and contractions as well as improper grammar. The multiple-choice section will also include questions that deal with sentence organization within a paragraph and paragraph organization. These questions will deal specifically with adding, deleting, rearranging, or substituting words and phrases in order to strengthen the text.

3. PART II—THE ESSAY SECTION

The second part of the Language Arts, Writing Test is the essay section. You will have 45 minutes to complete a 200–300 word essay on a topic that will be provided for you; you should set your target length at 250 words. Don't worry that you do not know the essay topic ahead of time. The test makers have designed the essay topic so that it measures your ability to express your thoughts and not to spontaneously write on some obscure topic. In fact, the essay topic will be one that you can write about based upon your own knowledge and personal experiences. This part of the test will measure your ability to organize your thoughts and write them in a way that the reader can easily understand and follow your thoughts and ideas. The readers of the essay will be looking for good organization of thoughts and ideas in the form of solid, well-organized, and well-written sentences and paragraphs. The readers will also be looking for proper grammar and usage within the essay. Because mastery of the English language is so important in creating good sentences and paragraphs (as on the essay part of the test) and is so important in detecting and correcting errors within text (as in the multiple-choice part of the test), let's do a quick review to refresh your memory of concepts and skills you'll need to be successful on the Language Arts, Writing Test.

4. PARTS OF SPEECH

All words within the English language fall into one of eight categories of words called the parts of speech. The parts of speech include nouns, pronouns, verbs, adjectives, adverbs, prepositions, conjunctions, and interjections. Let's take a look at each part of speech.

A **noun** is word that names a person, place, thing, or idea. A proper noun is a noun that must be capitalized because it is a proper name. A common noun is any noun that is not a proper noun. Nouns can be singular or plural. Nouns are the words that are almost always used as the subject of a sentence. All of the underlined words in the sentences below are nouns. If the nouns are capitalized, they are proper nouns.

The <u>boy</u> went to the <u>store</u> to buy some <u>milk</u>.

Her <u>sister</u> is getting married to <u>Tom</u> on <u>Friday</u> at the <u>church</u>.

These <u>birds</u> fly to <u>Florida</u> every <u>winter</u>.

A **pronoun** is a word that replaces or takes the place of a noun. Pronouns include words like *he*, *she*, *him*, *they*, or *it*. Pronouns can be singular or plural. All of the underlined words in the sentences below are pronouns.

<u>We</u> went with <u>them</u> to see the movie.

<u>It</u> was much longer than <u>he</u> expected.

A **verb** is a word that shows what another word is doing; in other words, a verb shows either action or being. An action verb, such as *walk* or *run*, expresses action, while a linking verb, such as *is*, *are*, *be*, or *was*, expresses a state of being. All of the underlined words below are verbs.

The car <u>drove</u> over the hill and through the woods.

Mr. Smith <u>talks</u> to Mr. Jones every day at the coffee shop.

Joe <u>is</u> a lawyer, and his father <u>was</u> a lawyer, too.

Verbs can be present tense, past tense, or future tense. In other words, a verb can show action that has happened, that is happening, or that will happen. Many times, a future tense verb is a compound verb or a combination of a verb and a helping verb such as *will*. The verb in the first sentence below is past tense, the verb in the second sentence is present tense, and the verb in third sentence is future tense.

The cat <u>jumped</u> over the fence.

The grass in the field <u>is</u> green.

I <u>will go</u> to the concert tomorrow.

An **adjective** is a word that describes, or modifies, a noun or a pronoun. In other words, an adjective provides a description of a noun or pronoun. Usually, an adjective comes just before the word that it describes. If two or more adjectives describe the same word, commas separate the adjectives. The underlined words in the sentences below are adjectives.

The <u>tall</u> man in the <u>yellow</u> suit drives a <u>beautiful</u> car.

My <u>crazy</u> uncle gave my mother a <u>funny</u>, <u>striped</u> hat.

The <u>big</u> jar of <u>purple</u> jelly is near the <u>small</u> carton of <u>chocolate</u> milk.

An **adverb** is similar to an adjective, but it describes or modifies a verb, an adjective, or another adverb. An adverb expresses time, place, or degree or answers questions such as *how much, how, when,* or *where.* Adverbs often end with the letters *-ly.* The underlined words in the sentences below are adverbs.

She <u>quickly</u> dropped the <u>very</u> hot potato.

Sam walked <u>slowly</u> down the street on an <u>unusually</u> cold day.

My computer <u>accurately</u> processes information.

A **preposition** is a word that links nouns, pronouns, and phrases. A preposition is said to introduce its object, which is the noun, pronoun, or phrase it modifies. Usually, a preposition indicates some kind of relationship between its object and the rest of the sentence. A good way to remember prepositions is to think about a table, as illustrated in the examples below. The underlined words in the sentences below are prepositions.

The cat ran <u>on</u> the table.

The cat ran <u>under</u> the table.

The cat ran <u>around</u> the table.

The cat ran <u>to</u> the table.

The cat ran <u>from</u> the table.

The cat ran <u>into</u> the table.

A **conjunction** is a word that joins or combines two other words, phrases, or clauses. The underlined words in the sentences below are conjunctions.

The dog <u>and</u> cat chased each other in the yard.

I like the movie, <u>but</u> I thought it was too long.

She went to college <u>after</u> she graduated from high school.

An **interjection** is a word that is added to a sentence for emphasis or to show emotion. An interjection is often punctuated with an exclamation point. The underlined words in the sentences below are interjections.

<u>Hey</u>! Put that down!

<u>Wow</u>, that is a big house!

<u>Ouch</u>, I just hit my thumb with a hammer!

5. SENTENCE STRUCTURE

Sentence structure is one of the most important areas that will be tested on the Language Arts, Writing Test. You will need to demonstrate your ability to use good sentence structure on the essay, and you will need to revise or correct sentences with poor sentence structure on the multiple-choice part of the test. Therefore, you must be familiar with proper sentence structure. A sentence is any group of words that expresses a complete thought or idea. A group of words that does not express a complete thought is called a sentence fragment; you want to avoid sentence fragments at all times when writing.

The first thing you need to know is that there are four kinds of sentences, including statements, commands, exclamations, and questions. Let's look at each one of these more closely. A statement is a sentence that simply gives information. A command gives orders. An exclamation shows feeling or emotion. A question makes an inquiry. Although they each have different purposes, each of the four types of sentences are fundamentally the same.

In writing, you can make sentences as simple or as complex as you would like, but all sentences have two things: a subject and a verb, sometimes referred to as a predicate. The subject of the sentence is the noun or pronoun that is talked about in the sentence. The verb, or predicate, tells what the subject is or does. In the sentences below, the subject is bold and the predicate is underlined.

The **fireman** <u>drove</u> quickly down the street.

The **politician** <u>kissed</u> the baby's cheek.

Many times, as in the sentences above, the subject comes before the verb. However, in a question, for example, the verb may come before the subject. In the sentences below, the subject is in bold and the verb is underlined.

<u>May</u> **I** <u>sit</u> down?

<u>Are</u> **you** <u>eating</u> pizza?

Also, some sentences have understood subjects that are not included in the sentence. In the sentences below, the understood subject is in parentheses and the verb is underlined.

(You) <u>Clean</u> the garage today.

(You) <u>Call</u> me when you get home tonight.

Because every sentence has a subject and a verb, it is important that the subject and verb agree. In other words, you must use a singular verb with a single subject, and you must use a plural verb with more than one subject. In the sentences below, the subject is bold and the verb is underlined. In the first sentence, the subject and verb do not agree. In the second sentence, the subject and verb agree.

The **trees** <u>grows</u> in the forest. (incorrect)

The **trees** <u>grow</u> in the forest. (correct)

Let's look at one more example of subject-verb agreement.

The **car** <u>drive</u> very nicely. (incorrect)

The **car** <u>drives</u> very nicely. (correct)

So far we have been looking at simple sentences, or sentences that have one subject and one verb. To increase the complexity of your sentences and make your writing better, you can add a few things to simple sentences. For example, by using a conjunction, you can make a sentence with two or more subjects. Be sure to make the verb agree with plural subjects. In the sentences below, the subjects are underlined.

The <u>car,</u> the <u>truck,</u> and the <u>boat</u> sat in the parking lot.

<u>Bill, Jim,</u> and <u>Frank</u> ate spaghetti last night.

You can also use a conjunction to join two verbs. In the sentences below, the verbs are underlined.

Sarah <u>sings</u> and <u>dances</u> in a local theater company.

The child <u>ran</u> and <u>played</u> for hours in the park.

By using a conjunction, you can add two simple sentences together to make a compound sentence.

When you write a compound sentence, be sure that the verb in each part of the sentence has the same tense. In the compound sentences below, the subjects are bold, the verbs are underlined, and the conjunction is in italic.

The **clowns** <u>are</u> funny, *and* the **lions** <u>are</u> scary.

This **building** <u>is</u> tall, *and* that **building** <u>is</u> short.

Sometimes you need to use a comma to punctuate a compound sentence, but be careful not to overuse commas. In the sentences below, notice the correct use of commas in the compound sentences.

He wants me to go to the dance, but I'll probably stay home.

It was snowing, yet I played outside all day.

Just as you must be aware of sentence fragments that do not express complete thoughts, you must also be aware of run-on sentences. A run-on sentence contains too much information and is organized in a way that makes understanding it very difficult. Often, a run-on sentence simply needs to be divided into two or more smaller sentences. The first sentence below is a run-on sentence. The second group of sentences is a revision of the first sentence.

We went to the mall shopped ate pizza and saw many people we knew who were shopping too.

We went to the mall, where we shopped and ate pizza. We saw many people we knew. They were shopping, too.

6. PARAGRAPHS

Once you have mastered the parts of speech and sentence structure, you are ready to construct good paragraphs. A good paragraph should be at least four or five sentences in length. Often, the main idea of the paragraph is located in the first sentence of the paragraph; this sentence is known as the topic sentence. Occasionally, the topic sentence will be at the end of the paragraph. The other sentences that make up the body of the paragraph should contain facts and details that support the topic sentence. If a sentence within a paragraph seems random and is not relevant to the topic sentence, it should be deleted. Extraneous facts and information distract the reader and make it harder for the reader to follow the thoughts being expressed in the paragraph. Each paragraph should be about a different topic, and paragraphs should not repeat what previous paragraphs have said.

In an essay or some longer work, paragraphs should flow together. Often, writers use transitional words and phrases to string paragraphs together in an essay. If a paragraph seems to begin in a strange way, it probably needs to be rewritten so that there is a smoother transition from one paragraph to the other. For example, a paragraph should not begin with words such as *but* or *and*.

7. PRACTICING LANGUAGE ARTS, WRITING QUESTIONS

Directions: Items 1-5 are based on the following document.

(1) Although many people think that a job interview are stressful and difficult, a job interview can be an exciting event. (2) The key to making the job interview process less stressful is confidence. (3) The applicant, must accept the challenge, of convincing the prospective employer that he is the best candidate for the job. (4) Nice cologne is a plus. (5) A person applying for a job should approach the prospective employer with a positive, winning attitude. (6) The applicant should explain what he has to offer to the prospective employer. (7) The applicant should promote himself and tout his strengths.

(8) And during the interview, the applicant should firmly shake the hand of the person interviewing him. (9) The applicant should look the prospective employer in the eye and maintain eye contact throughout the interview. (10) The applicant should concentrate about the questions and an-

swer them confidently. (11) When answering questions, the applicant should avoid fidgeting and stuttering. (12) At the conclusion of the interview, the applicant should tell the interviewer that he appreciates the opportunity and that he looks forward to another conversation at a later date.

1. Sentence (1) Although many people think that a job interview are stressful and difficult, a job interview can be an exciting event.

   Which of the following corrections should be made?

   (1) Change <u>Although</u> to <u>Because</u>
   (2) Change <u>interview are</u> to <u>interview is</u>
   (3) Delete the comma
   (4) Change <u>be</u> to <u>is</u>
   (5) No correction is necessary

2. Sentence (3) The applicant, must accept the challenge, of convincing the prospective employer that he is the best candidate for the job.

   Which of the following corrections can be made?

   (1) Change <u>applicant</u> to <u>applicants</u>
   (2) Delete the commas
   (3) Add a comma after <u>candidate</u>
   (4) Change <u>prospective</u> to <u>perspective</u>
   (5) No correction is necessary

3. Sentence (4) Nice cologne is a plus.

   Which of the following corrections can be made?

   (1) Change <u>Nice</u> to <u>Really nice</u>
   (2) Change <u>is</u> to <u>are</u>
   (3) Change <u>plus</u> to <u>positive</u>
   (4) Delete the sentence
   (5) No correction is necessary

4. Sentence (8) And during the interview, the applicant should firmly shake the hand of the person interviewing him.

   Which of the following corrections can be made?

   (1) Delete <u>And</u>
   (2) Add a comma after <u>applicant</u>
   (3) Change <u>interviewing</u> to <u>that interviewed</u>
   (4) Remove <u>should</u>
   (5) No correction is necessary

5. Sentence (10) The applicant should concentrate about the questions and answer them confidently.

   Which of the following corrections can be made?

   (1) Change <u>concentrate</u> to <u>consecrate</u>
   (2) Change <u>about</u> to <u>on</u>
   (3) Change <u>them</u> to <u>then</u>
   (4) Add <u>with</u> after <u>them</u>
   (5) No correction is necessary

Answer Explanations

1. **The correct answer is (2).** The subject and verb must agree.

2. **The correct answer is (2).** This sentence does not need commas.

3. **The correct answer is (4).** This sentence is irrelevant to the rest of the paragraph.

4. **The correct answer is (1).** The first sentence of a paragraph should not begin with *and*.

5. **The correct answer is (2).** *On* is the correct preposition to use in this sentence.

Day 11

Sharpening Your Writing Skills

Topics for today:

1. Introduction to writing
2. Organizing your thoughts
3. Forming a five-paragraph essay
4. Tips and strategies for improving your writing

1. INTRODUCTION TO WRITING

One of the most important skills that the GED will measure is your ability to express your thoughts through writing. Writing is probably something you do every day without giving it much thought. Whether you write letters, e-mails, or memos, you know that writing is simply putting your thoughts into written form. Some people get intimidated when they are required to write a formal essay that will be read and graded by someone. You shouldn't be intimidated at all, though. Writing for the GED is not much different than the writing you do all the time. There are really only a few simple things that you will need to remember when your write your essay for the GED. Let's start with the very first thing that you should do when you receive the topic for the essay section of the Language Arts, Writing Test.

2. ORGANIZING YOUR THOUGHTS

As you have already learned, the Language Arts, Writing Test will have a section in which you will

write an essay on a topic that is provided for you. You will not know ahead of time what the topic is going to be, but the essay topic is not something that you should worry about. The writers of the GED are not going to try to stump or confuse you by giving you an obscure topic about which you will need to know many trivial facts or details. On the contrary, the writers of the GED will try to choose a topic that is very open-ended and that will allow you to write freely based on your knowledge and life experiences. After all, the Language Arts, Writing Test is designed to measure your ability to write and not your ability to recall facts about obscure topics.

The first thing that a test taker may be tempted to do when he reads the topic for the essay is to start writing off the top of his head. That same test taker may be worried about completing his essay in the allotted time so he may just jump right into the writing. This is not the recommended procedure, though. If you just start writing without plotting your course first, your essay may be unorganized and muddled. Organization of your thoughts will be one of the most important things that you will be expected to demonstrate on the Language Arts, Writing Test. The first thing you should do when you read the essay topic is take a minute or 2 to stop and think. You will have plenty of time for writing, so take just a minute and think about what you want to say in your essay. You will be much more productive and efficient if you have a well-thought-out plan for writing than if you just start writing with no plan at all.

In the first few minutes after you receive your essay topic, organize your thoughts. First, think about the overall point that you want to make in your essay. The point that you want to make should be the theme, or main idea, throughout your essay. After you have decided on the theme for your essay, think about what smaller points you can make to support the main idea of your essay. These smaller points will make up the body of your essay. After you have decided on the main idea and the supporting facts and details for your essay, you are ready to develop an outline.

3. FORMING A FIVE-PARAGRAPH ESSAY

Once you have organized your thoughts and have decided which direction your are going to go with your essay, you are ready to form an outline. This outline will help you write a good, solid five-paragraph essay. Also, this outline should keep you on target for your goal of approximately 250 words in the 45 minutes you are given to write the essay. The outline should like this:

I.   Introductory paragraph

II.   Supporting Paragraph 1

III.   Supporting Paragraph 2

IV.   Supporting Paragraph 3

V.   Conclusion

This simple outline will keep you focused and help prevent you from straying from the point that you are trying to make with your essay. Let's look a little closer at the role of each paragraph.

First, let's look at the introductory paragraph. The purpose of the introductory paragraph is to introduce the reader to the main idea of the essay. In other words, you should use the introductory paragraph to tell the reader what you are going to say in the body of your essay. In the introductory paragraph, present the main idea of the essay along with a brief statement of each of the supporting points for your main idea. This will provide focus and direction for the rest of your essay.

Next, you should write the first of three supporting paragraphs. Whether you are giving a speech or writing an essay, a good rule of thumb is to make three points of emphasis. By having three points, you get an opportunity to adequately express yourself. At the same time, though, having three points will keep you focused and keep the interest of the audience. Each of the three supporting paragraphs should be based on one of the points that you are using to support the main idea of the essay. At the beginning of each supporting paragraph, you should write that paragraph's topic sentence. The topic sentence of the paragraph is one of the supporting points for the main idea of the essay and is the main idea for that particular paragraph. Each sentence in the paragraph should then support the topic sentence of the paragraph.

Finally, after you have written the three supporting paragraphs, you should write the conclusion. The conclusion is the paragraph in which you wrap up your thoughts and sum up your essay. In other words, briefly recap for the reader the information that you just presented to her. It is important to develop a good conclusion so the reader is not left hanging at the end of the essay. Be sure that your conclusion is concise and does not ramble. Restate your points and conclude the essay. If you follow this formula, you will be successful in developing your essay.

4. TIPS AND STRATEGIES FOR IMPROVING YOUR WRITING

Let's take a look at a few tips and strategies for improving your essay. Often, these few simple strategies will be the difference between a good essay and an excellent essay.

Be consistent with your paragraphs and sentences. When writing sentences, try not to make them too long or too short. They do not have to be fancy or complex sentences to make your point. Likewise, keep your paragraphs a reasonable length. A good paragraph will include between four and six good sentences. Remember to keep the length and complexity of your paragraphs and sentences consistent throughout your essay.

Keep your writing focused. When writing your essay, keep your paragraphs and sentences focused on the main idea. Don't let your sentences wander off the topic on a wild goose chase. When you keep your writing focused on the main idea, you keep the reader interested, you make your point more effectively, and you keep the quality of your writing high.

Concentrate on spelling and grammar. Make an effort to use proper grammar in your sentences. Sentence fragments and run-on sentences significantly weaken your writing. Besides simply demonstrating your mastery of language skills, the use of proper grammar in your writing will give your writing credibility. The same holds true with spelling. Good spelling will also add credibility. A general rule to follow is if you don't know how to spell a word, think of another word that means the same thing. This little bit of extra effort will go a long way to making your essay better. After all, would you rather read something written correctly or something full of spelling and grammar errors?

Be confident in your writing. When you write your essay, your job is to make a statement. Therefore, you should avoid saying things like "maybe," "perhaps," or "I'm not sure." Instead, take a positive approach and let the reader know that you have a good knowledge of your subject.

Avoid using superlatives and emotional language. Keep your writing unemotional and avoid using superlatives. Superlatives are words such as *best, worst, greatest, of all time,* or *in all of history.* These words and phrases are difficult, if not impossible, to defend or support in a short essay. Also, avoid using strong emotional language such as *I hate* or *I love.* Even if you are expressing your opinion or your point of view, these phrases make it difficult to present a factual, to-the-point essay.

Keep it simple. Simple, concise, and to-the-point paragraphs and sentences can convey a message just as well as long, fancy paragraphs and sentences. There is no need to complicate your writing by trying to impress the reader. Keeping it simple will help you stay focused and make your point efficiently and effectively. Remember that quality is better than quantity when you are writing.

Day 12

Preparing for Social Studies

Topics for today:

1. Introduction to the Social Studies Test
2. History on the Social Studies Test
3. Political Science on the Social Studies Test
4. Economics on the Social Studies Test
5. Geography on the Social Studies Test
6. Documents on the Social Studies Test
7. Practicing Social Studies Questions

1. INTRODUCTION TO THE SOCIAL STUDIES TEST

The Social Studies Test contains 50 questions that you will have 75 minutes to answer. A little more than half of the Social Studies Test questions will be based on reading passages of up to approximately 250 words in length. The remaining questions will be based on visuals such as charts, graphs, tables, maps, or political cartoons. The Social Studies Test includes questions from history, economics, political science, and geography. The key to success on the Social Studies Test is not the amount of historical or other social studies related information you know but rather your ability to comprehend and analyze what you read or see. Although knowledge of the four social studies fields certainly will be helpful, you will probably do well on this test with just your ability to comprehend and analyze written and visual information. This chapter will outline the most important social studies information to complement your comprehension skills. A good balance of social studies knowledge and comprehension skills will be a terrific recipe for success on the Social Studies Test. For a more thorough examination of the Social Studies Test, refer to ARCO's *Master the GED—Social Studies* also published by Arco. Let's briefly revisit some strategies you should use on the Social Studies Test.

Remember that the majority of questions will be based on information documents or reading passages, so we'll begin by looking at strategies for those questions. First, when you read the reading passages, remember to look for the main idea of the reading passage; it is often located in the first sentence of a paragraph. Next, try to find clues that will help determine the context of the passage as well as the author and the intended audience. Finally, look for any names, terms, or topics that you recognize as significant or important. These clues will help you comprehend and analyze the text so that you can correctly answer the questions. Now let's look at some strategies to help with the visuals. First, read the title or caption of the visual; often the title or caption will offer a clue as to the meaning or purpose of the visual. If the visual is a cartoon, closely examine the cartoon for any recognizable images. If you recognize anyone or anything in the cartoon, you will probably have little trouble answering the questions. If you don't recognize anything in the cartoon, the title, caption, dialogue in the cartoon, or action in the cartoon will offer the clues you need to interpret it. If the visual is a map, chart, table, or graph, the title or caption will help you understand the purpose of the visual. Survey the information presented in the visual and then read the question. This will help identify exactly what you will be looking for in the visual.

2. HISTORY ON THE SOCIAL STUDIES TEST

History questions will make up more of the Social Studies Test than any other kind of questions. The history questions will not test random names, dates, facts, or other trivial information. Rather, the history questions will measure your ability to work with and glean information from historical documents and visuals. If you have a good background in U.S. (or Canadian) history, you will have a good advantage on the Social Studies Test. If you have good comprehension and analytical skills, you will have a huge advantage on the Social Studies Test. Let's look at some of the most important information you need to know from the area of history on the Social Studies Test. What follows is a summary of the history of the United States and then a summary of the history of Canada, highlighting the most significant trends and events.

United States History

In the 1400s and 1500s, Europeans began exploring and settling on the continents of North America and South America. By 1700, the French, British, Spanish, and Portuguese had established colonies somewhere in the New World. The English and French became the dominant forces along the eastern seaboard of North America. The thirteen British colonies on the eastern coast grew and developed their own identity and interests. As they grew, they became less and less dependent on Britain. By the 1770s, many colonists desired a break from the control of Britain and wanted control over their own affairs. High taxes and unfair representation fueled the colonists' desire for independence. In 1776, the colonies declared themselves independent and free from the rule of Britain with the Declaration of Independence. The British king did not want to let the colonies break away, so he sent troops to put down the rebellion in the colonies. The War for American Independence, or American Revolution, had begun. After much fighting between the American colonists and the British, troops the colonists, with the help of France and other foreign countries, finally won their freedom from Britain. In 1783, the two countries signed the Treaty of Paris, which recognized the United States.

The loose confederation of states adopted the Constitution, or written plan of government, in 1787 and added ten amendments, or additions, in 1791 that became known as the Bill of Rights. As the nation grew, people debated over the general direction in which the nation should go. The two sides in the debate grew into early political parties, the Republicans and the Federalists. During the first few decades, the American people expressed their desire to govern themselves by supporting the parties and candidates that favored a limited central government and stronger state governments.

Under the leadership of President Thomas Jefferson, the small nation began expanding westward with the Louisiana Purchase. Despite the harsh conditions and Native Americans who did not want to give up their homeland, American settlers pushed westward and eventually formed fourteen more states in the Louisiana Purchase territories. The United States also tried to expand its trade during this time. The trade policies of the United States angered the British, and the two nations again went to war in the War of 1812. Although the United States won the war, the war settled nothing. After the war, the nation continued its westward expansion toward the Pacific Ocean. After the war, the economy of the nation also began to grow. The North developed an industrial economy, and the South developed an agricultural economy. Economic rivalry and differences in opinions on such issues as slavery drove a wedge between the two regions. After the election of Abraham Lincoln as President in 1860, the Southern states seceded, or withdrew, from the Union. President Lincoln, in order to preserve the Union, used the military to bring the Southern states back into the fold. The bloody U.S. Civil War, which was won by the North, resulted in the preservation of the Union and the readmission of the Southern states into the United States. In addition, slavery was banned throughout the United States. After the war, the U.S. entered a tense era known as Reconstruction during which the nation tried to rebuild itself. This era was marked by much resentment between the North and South.

After the war, the entire country entered a period of industrialization and expansion of factories. This was a time of economic growth and prosperity in the United States. Railroads were added across the country, and people flocked to cities everywhere in search of work. Big businesses and corporations flourished. By the end of the 1800s, many businesses and government agencies had become corrupt and the people called for reform, or change. At the end of the century, the United States went to war with Spain and won more territories. The United States moved into the 1900s as an up-and-coming world power.

Despite new efforts to stay out of war, the United States entered World War I, known then as the Great War, in the early twentieth century to help the Triple Entente (Great Britain, France, and Russia) defend themselves against an aggressive Germany. The U.S. turned the tide of the war and helped defeat Germany. In the decade after World War I known as the Roaring 20s, the United States experienced an economic boom. The boom did not last, though, and the U.S., along with much of the world, faced the Great Depression at the end of the 1920s and throughout much of the 1930s. When the United States entered World War II in 1941, the country climbed out of depression. As in World War I, the United States emerged victorious. The United States had established itself as a legitimate superpower. The last half of the twentieth century saw the United States involved in a Cold War with the Soviet Union and other communist countries. As the end of the century approached, tensions eased and communist governments collapsed. By the end of the twentieth century, the United States had proven itself as an economic and military leader in the world.

Canadian History

The first Europeans to make contact with Canada probably arrived in the late 900s. The Vikings established a few settlements and maintained contact for some time. However, by the 1400s, Europeans probably had little or no contact any longer with Canada. As the Europeans began to explore again at the end of the century, exploration and settlement of Canada resumed. The Europeans first sought a route to Asia through Canada but eventually settled there as a result of the vast natural resources, including fish and furs. The French and British became the dominant forces in the region and each established colonies along the eastern coast of Canada. The Europeans maintained fairly cordial relations with the natives of Canada. However, diseases brought by the Europeans eventually sent the native population into a decline.

The British and French engaged each other in a few small wars through the years, but nothing major ever came of the wars. By the late 1700s, though, the tension between the French and British erupted into a major war known as the French and Indian War or the Seven Years War. Ultimately, Britain won the war, and France ceded its territory to Great Britain. The British struggled to establish their rule in Canada, especially in Quebec, because of the large numbers of Canadians who were French. Britain eventually divided Canada into sections that helped ease the tensions for a while. In the early 1800s, the United States tried to take advantage of its proximity to Canada. During the War of 1812, the U.S. unsuccessfully attempted to take parts of Canada. This created a great deal of anti-American sentiment in Canada.

During the 1800s, trading companies moved westward through Canada toward the Pacific in search of more natural resources. As the traders explored and settled the frontier, immigrants from other countries moved to Canada in search of economic opportunities. By the end of the 1800s, the natives of Canada had become the minority there. Also during the 1800s, many people across Canada called for reform of the government. After an armed rebellion in Canada, Britain officially created the province of Canada and divided it into sections, each with representation. Eventually, other provinces were created, too. The provinces controlled local affairs, and Britain controlled foreign policy. Later in the century, Canada became a confederation, and British troops left Canada for good. However, Canada still maintained political ties to Britain. As the end of the century drew to a close, Canada entered an industrial era that saw railroads, factories, and telegraph lines constructed across Canada. This era was a transition from the fishing and farming ways of early Canada to the industrial ways of modern Canada.

During the 1900s, Canada maintained close ties to Britain by supporting the British war efforts in World War I. After the war, Britain granted Canada the right to act as a sovereign state but under a British monarch. Canada endured the Great Depression along with rest of the world and, likewise, began to emerge from the depression with the onset of World War II. After the war, the greatest challenge that faced Canada was the issue of Quebec. Quebec, a French-speaking and historically French province, repeatedly pushed for independence from the very-British Canada. Often, the struggle resulted in violence. To this day, the independence of Quebec remains a topic of much debate.

3. POLITICAL SCIENCE ON THE SOCIAL STUDIES TEST

Basically, political science is the study of governments and methods of governing. The political science questions on the Social Studies Test will cover systems of government as well as information that is specific to the governments of the United States or Canada. As with the history questions, the political science questions will measure your ability to comprehend and analyze documents and visuals relating to political science. The political science questions will not test your recall of facts and figures.

Let's begin with the basic political systems of the world. A democracy is a government that is ruled by the people. In other words, in a democracy, the people make the important decisions. A similar government is a republic. In a republic, the people place the power to make decisions in the hands of elected representatives. An aristocracy is a government in which the elite of society have the power to rule. In an oligarchy, a few people have the power to rule; usually these people have used the military to gain power. A monarchy is a government headed by a single ruler, either a king or queen. A dictatorship is another government ruled by one person. However, a dictator usually assumes power with the military and rules with absolute power afterward. A total lack of government is called anarchy.

The United States has chosen a republic as its form of government. The United States government is also called a federal government because it divides its powers between national, state, and local governments. At each of those levels of government, the responsibilities have been divided among three separate branches of government. These branches are the legislative branch, the executive branch, and the judicial branch. The legislative branch makes the laws, the executive branch carries out the laws, and the judicial branch interprets the laws. At the national level, the legislative branch consists of the Senate and the House of Representatives. The president is the head of the executive branch, and he oversees all the agencies that carry out and enforce the laws. The Supreme Court is the highest level of the nation's judicial branch. Most states have a government similar to that of the national government. At the state level, most legislatures include a Senate and a House of Representatives, and a governor is the head of the executive branch. The judicial branch varies from state to state, but most states have a Supreme Court. In some cases, though, the state's judicial branch has two highest courts, one for civil cases and one for criminal cases. At the local level, most cities and municipalities have three branches of government. These branches of government vary widely, though, from place to place.

Canada has chosen a constitutional monarchy as its government. A constitutional monarchy is one in which a monarch, the queen in this case, rules but the monarch's power is limited by the country's constitution. The powers of the government are shared between the national, provincial, and local governments, thus making the Canadian government a federal government. Like the United States, Canada has three separate branches of government at each of the three levels. Like the United States, the three branches are the legislative, executive, and judicial branches. The head of the executive branch is the Governor General. The legislative branch consists of the House of Commons and the Senate. The highest court in Canada is the Supreme Court, the last resort for all appeals in the Canadian judiciary. At the provincial level, a Lieutenant Governor heads the executive branch, while a Commissioner heads the executive branch in the territories. The provincial and municipal levels of government also have judiciaries and legislatures that share government authority.

4. ECONOMICS ON THE SOCIAL STUDIES TEST

Economics is the study of the way society uses limited material resources to meet its material needs. The two branches of economics are microeconomics and macroeconomics. Microeconomics, also known as price theory, examines how supply, demand, and competition cause differences in prices, profits, wages, and other aspects of economics. Macroeconomics looks at the larger picture of economics and examines such things as employment and national income. There are a few major economic systems that exist in the world today just as there are a number of political systems. The most common economic systems are capitalism, socialism, and communism. Capitalism is an economic system in which private ownership of material resources, or capital, is not only allowed but also encouraged. In the economic system known as socialism, the government is in charge of the redistribution of wealth and the major industries are either owned publicly or cooperatively. In a communist economic system, the government does not permit private ownership of either capital or the means of production. A communist government owns the property within the state and determines the way the goods and services should be distributed.

The most important concept within the field of economics is that of supply and demand. Supply refers to all available goods, and demand refers to the desire of consumers to purchase goods. According to the principle of supply and demand, the price of goods increases if either the supply of those goods decreases or if the consumer demand increases. Conversely, the price of goods decreases if either the supply increases too much or if the consumer demand decreases. Supply and demand can be charted as in the figure below.

Another major concept of economics has to do with the factors of production. These factors are natu-

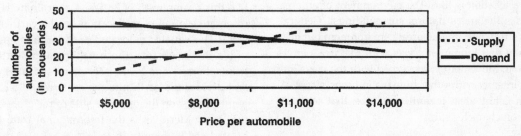

Supply and Demand Chart for Automobiles. Notice that the supply of automobiles is higher when the price is higher. Conversely, the demand for automobiles is higher when the price is lower.

ral resources, capital, and labor. Natural resources are the raw materials necessary for the production of goods. Capital can be any equipment, factories, or property necessary for the conversion of raw materials into finished goods. In economics, the term *labor* is used to describe the work it takes to convert raw materials into goods and services. Labor may refer to the people who actually do the work manufacturing the raw materials and producing the goods.

In most nations, the government plays a major role in steering the economy through fiscal policy and monetary policy. Fiscal policy involves both the control of taxation and control of spending in such programs as welfare and unemployment benefits. Monetary policy involves the printing and distributing of money as well as control of the amount of money available for use by banks and consumers. Governments can use many methods to help stimulate or slow the economy. Governments can also do a number of things to control inflation, or the general rise in prices.

5. GEOGRAPHY ON THE SOCIAL STUDIES TEST

Geography is more than the study of maps and states and capitals. Geography is the study of the earth's physical features and the way man has adapted to these physical features. Vital to the study of geography is an understanding of the five themes of geography: location, place, environment, movement, and region. In geography, location means an exact and precise position on the earth's surface. Place means not only where a location is but also what a location is like. The environment of an area includes the area's natural surroundings. Geographers study not only an area's environment but also the way that humans interact with the area's environment. Movement is concerned with the ways humans interact with other humans in other places. A region is any area, regardless of size, that contains common characteristics.

Two of the most important tools used by geographers and students of geography are maps and globes. Because the earth is round, a flat representation of the earth is inaccurate; therefore, a globe is the most accurate way to study the earth's surface. However, a globe is not the most efficient or convenient vehicle for geographical information. Therefore, geographers most often rely on the flat representations of the earth's surface known as maps. There are several different kinds of maps that geographers use: political, topographical, contour, population, and weather. A political map shows political borders or boundaries between countries, states, and counties. A topographical map illustrates physical features such as mountains, hills, valleys, rivers, or prairies. A contour map illustrates the elevation of physical features. A population map illustrates population density or how many people live in a particular area. A weather map, or climate map, illustrates the forecasted or current weather for an area. Regardless of the kind of map you may be studying, the map key or legend, usually found in one of the corners of the map, will explain the meanings of the symbols on the map as well as the scale that is used for the map.

To find an exact location on a map or a globe, geographers use imaginary lines called latitude lines and longitude lines that run around the earth. *Latitude lines* run east and west around the earth and measure distances north and south of the equator. *Longitude lines* run north and south around the earth and measure distances east and west of the equator. Both latitude and longitude are measured in degrees. The intersection of a latitude line and a longitude line is called a coordinate and is written like this example: 45°N 88°W. A coordinate is representative of an exact location on the earth's surface. The equator is located at 0° latitude and divides the earth into the northern and southern hemispheres. The Prime Meridian is located at 0° and divides the earth into the eastern and western hemispheres; on the opposite side of the globe from the Prime Meridian is the International Date Line, located at 180° longitude.

6. DOCUMENTS ON THE SOCIAL STUDIES TEST

At least one of the reading passages on the Social Studies Test will be from one of the following historical documents: the Declaration of Independence, the U.S. Constitution, the Federalist Papers, and landmark Supreme Court cases. The question or questions based on such a reading passage will measure your ability to comprehend the document. The Declaration of Independence, written in 1776, declared the thirteen colonies free and independent of British rule. The U.S. Constitution outlines the basic plan for the United States government. The Federalist Papers, written by John Jay, James Madison, and Alexander Hamilton, were written before the ratification of the Constitution in an attempt to persuade people to accept the Constitution. The landmark Supreme Court cases could be any cases that have been decided by the Supreme Court and have impacted U.S. history.

7. PRACTICING SOCIALS STUDIES QUESTIONS

Directions: Items 1 and 2 are based on the following document.

"The ostensible cause of the war was the issue of slavery. However, slavery was just one of many issues that drove a wedge between the two sides. One of the main points of contention between the two sides was the issue of states' rights. Another issue was the blatant favoritism shown in Congress toward one region instead of another. The final straw, though, was the election of Abraham Lincoln, a candidate who did not even receive a true mandate of the people based on the number of votes he received."

1. The war referred to in the paragraph above is which of the following?
    (1) War for American Independence
    (2) War of 1812
    (3) French and Indian War
    (4) U.S. Civil War
    (5) Spanish-American War

2. Which of the following can be said about the passage?
    (1) The author of the document most likely sympathized with the South.
    (2) The author of the document most likely sympathized with the North.
    (3) The passage was written immediately after the war.
    (4) The passage was written many years after the war.
    (5) The passage was written by a war scholar.

Directions: Item 3 refers to the following passage.

"We the people of the United States, in order to form a more perfect union, establish justice, insure domestic tranquillity, provide for the common defense, promote the general welfare, and secure the blessings of liberty to ourselves and our posterity, do ordain and establish this Constitution for the United States of America."

3. The passage above is most likely an excerpt from which of the following documents?
    (1) Declaration of Independence
    (2) Federalist Paper #17
    (3) U.S. Constitution
    (4) U.S. Supreme Court case *Roe v. Wade*
    (5) U.S. Supreme Court case *Marbury v. Madison*

Directions: Item 4 refers to the following passage.

"Private ownership of heavy industry or corporations is not allowed. Heavy industry will be operated by the state. Additionally, health care, education and banking will fall under the control of the state. Redistribution of resources will be the responsibility of the state."

4. The passage above most accurately describes which of the following economic systems?

(1) Capitalism

(2) Socialism

(3) Communism

(4) Anarchism

(5) A mixed economy

Directions: Item 5 refers to the following map.

5. The map above is an example of which of the following?

(1) Topographical map

(2) Contour map

(3) Political map

(4) Globe

(5) Weather map

Answer Explanations

1. **The correct answer is (4).** The context clues within the passage, *slavery* and *Abraham Lincoln* for example, indicate the passage is about the U.S. Civil War.

2. **The correct answer is (1).** Because of the tone of the passage, it is reasonable to assume the author sympathized with the South.

3. **The correct answer is (3).** The passage mentions the establishment of the Constitution.

4. **The correct answer is (3).** The passage describes several characteristics of a communist state.

5. **The correct answer is (3).** The map depicts boundaries and areas affected by political agreements and diplomacy, thus making it a political map.

Day 13

Preparing for Science

Topics for today:

1. Introduction to the Science Test
2. Life Science on the Science Test
3. Earth Science on the Science Test
4. Physical Science on the Science Test
5. Practicing Science Questions

1. INTRODUCTION TO THE SCIENCE TEST

The Science Test will contain 50 questions that you will have 80 minutes to answer. The questions will measure your ability to understand and interpret scientific information. Some of the questions will be based on reading passages, some will be based on visuals, and some will be single set items. The questions cover three areas of science that include life science, earth and space science, and physical science. Of the questions on the Science Test, 45 percent of the questions will be based on Life Science, 20 percent on Earth and Space Science, and 35 percent on Physical Science. This will be a brief review of the most important information and concepts you will need to know for the science test. For a complete and more thorough review, refer to *Master the GED—Science*, also by ARCO.

2. LIFE SCIENCE ON THE SCIENCE TEST

Life Science, or biology, is the study of living organisms. The most basic level of living things is the cell. Some organisms are unicellular (contain only one cell), while others are multicellular (contain many cells). Cells come in many shapes and sizes, but they almost all share a few characteristics. First, a cell must have a cell membrane that keeps the cell in and everything else out of the cell. The cell membrane is usually semipermeable. This means that the membrane lets in some things and keeps other things out. Inside the cell membrane is the cytoplasm, a substance that contains all other cell structures. Cells with a nucleus are called eukaryotes, while cells without a nucleus are called prokaryotes. The nucleus is basically the control center for all that happens inside the cell. The main difference between plant cells and animal cells is that plant cells have a cell wall and animal cells do not. Another difference between plant and animal cells is the way that the cells get energy. A plant cell gets its energy from a process called photosynthesis. In photosynthesis, the chloroplasts in the plant cells capture light, carbon dioxide, and water and then turn those into oxygen and glucose, or sugar. These sugars are stored in the plant. In an animal cell, nutrients pass through the cell membrane and into the proper part of the cell.

Each cell has a certain code that contains information about the traits it will have. These traits are determined by chromosomes, and the study of how these traits are passed on is called *genetics*. The chromosomes are located in the nuclei of the cells and made up of genes, or pieces of DNA. This is the genetic blueprint for the way the cells, and ultimately the organism, will develop. An organism's genes determine which traits will be passed from one generation to the next. The passing of traits to offspring is called *heredity*.

As you have already learned, cells are the smallest unit of life. In an animal, groups of similar cells join together to form tissues. Groups of similar tissues form organs that perform certain functions. The stomach and the lungs are good examples of organs. Groups of organs that work together in an organism are called *systems*. For example, the stomach and the intestines make up the digestive system. The cells, tissues, organs, and systems make up organisms.

Living organisms are grouped together, or classified, based on similarities. The largest grouping is known as a *kingdom*. All living things are in one of two kingdoms, plant or animal. The kingdoms are then subdivided into smaller groups called *phylum, class, order, family, genus*, and *species*. The organisms within each smaller subdivision contain an increasing number of similarities. Therefore, the organisms within any given family will have many more similarities than organisms within a phylum.

Many organisms are not the same today as they were many, many years ago. Various changes in an organism's environment may cause the organism to change in order to survive. This change is called *evolution*. In evolution, organisms usually change from simpler organisms to more complex organisms. Change that occurs in order for an organism to better fit into its environment is called *adaptation*. When these changes occur over a long period of time, scientists refer to the process as natural selection. The organisms that adapt and evolve are the organisms that survive.

Organisms of the same species that live together and reproduce together in a given area make up what scientists refer to as a population. A group of populations is known as a community. There may dozens of different populations within a given community. A community and its environment make up an ecosystem. Ecosystems can range in size from the biosphere, or all of the communities on Earth, to a fish tank in a classroom. Within each ecosystem, there are producers, or organisms that produce energy, and consumers, or organisms that depend on consumers for energy. The system of consumers eating producers within an ecosystem is called a food web or food chain. This is the way that energy is passed along within an ecosystem. Energy may be in the form of oxygen, water, sugars, or something else vital to the life of the consumers.

3. EARTH AND SPACE SCIENCE ON THE SCIENCE TEST

The earth is a mostly spherical planet that is slightly flattened at the North and South Poles and slightly bulging at the equator. The earth is made up of three layers—the crust, or outer layer; the mantle, which lies below the crust; and the core, or the innermost layer of the earth. The core has two layers of its own, the inner and outer cores. The earth's crust is the part of the earth on which we live. Its many landforms and its movement can be explained through the theory of plate tectonics. This theory says that there are tectonic plates that make up the earth's crust. These plates are not permanent in location. These plates move around, several inches each year in some cases. At the boundary between two plates, landforms and earthquakes often occur. As the plates collide, the crust is thrust upward, forming hills and mountains. As the plates separate, molten material rises up from the mantle to form new crust. Some plates simply move past one another without creating or destroying new crust. These boundaries are called fault lines and are prime locations for earthquakes.

Above the earth's surface is the atmosphere. The atmosphere contains numerous levels and contains the air that we breathe. The atmosphere is also where weather takes place. All weather is caused by uneven heating and cooling of the earth. The uneven heating and cooling causes movement of cold air and warm air. Warm air from the equator rises, while cold air from the poles sinks. This causes prevailing winds around the earth. Uneven heating also causes ocean currents, another natural pattern that affects weather. Daily weather is caused by the movement of air masses, some warm and some cold. Where two air masses meet, it is known as a front. When a cold air mass displaces warm air, a cold front occurs. Conversely, when warm air rises above cold air, a warm front occurs. It is common for clouds and precipitation, or moisture that falls to the earth, to accompany fronts. The study of weather is called *meteorology*. Weather patterns over an extended period of time are referred to as climate.

The solar system includes the sun, which is a star; nine planets; and the planets' satellites, or moons. The solar system also includes an asteroid belt. The nine planets include (listed in order of proximity to the sun) Mercury, Venus, Earth, Mars, Jupiter, Saturn, Uranus, Neptune, and Pluto. The four planets closest to the sun are rocky planets called the inner planets and are relatively small. The five planets farthest from the sun are the outer planets. With the exception of Pluto, the outer planets are large planets of gas. All of the planets except for Mercury and Venus have at least one satellite, or moon, in its orbit. The solar system is part of a larger group of stars called a galaxy. The galaxy in which our solar system is found is the Milky Way. Galaxies have millions or trillions of stars along with gases and dust. Galaxies are held together in much the same way that gravity holds planets in a solar system or the way gravity holds a moon in a planet's orbit. The Milky Way is one of 27 galaxies in the Local Group. There may be an infinite number of galaxies in our universe.

The sun is one of an infinite number of stars in the universe. The sun is a medium-sized star called a yellow star made mostly of helium and hydrogen. After billions of years, a yellow star may run low on hydrogen and may become a red giant. Eventually, a red giant may collapse and explode. The result would be a supernova and then a neutron star. Gravity might then cause the neutron star to collapse on itself and leave a black hole, a phenomenon whose gravity is so great that even light cannot escape. However, if a red giant were to slowly lose mass, it would become a white dwarf.

The study of the stars and other heavenly objects is known as astronomy. The study of the origins of the universe is known as cosmology. Cosmologists have a number of theories about the origins of the universe, but the one that may be most widely accepted is that of the Big Bang. According to this theory, the entire universe began long ago as a small, extremely dense mass. The Big Bang, or an explosion, caused all of the extremely dense matter to be hurled outward into space. Though the Big Bang theory is a topic of much debate, scientists have discovered some evidence that supports the Big Bang theory.

4. PHYSICAL SCIENCE ON THE SCIENCE TEST

The basic building block for all matter is a particle called the atom. However, atoms are made up of subatomic particles called protons, neutrons, and electrons. Positively charged protons and neutrons with no charge make up the nucleus of an atom. Negatively charged electrons orbit the nucleus of the atom. If an atom has the same number of protons and electrons, the atom has a neutral charge. If an atom gains or loses electrons, it becomes a negative or positive ion. The most basic substances that are made up of only similar atoms are called elements. Hydrogen, helium, silver, and lead are all examples of elements. Each element has a chemical symbol and a place on the Periodic Table of Elements. Compounds are substances that are composed of two or more elements that have been chemically combined. Each compound can be written as a chemical formula. For example, salt can be written as $NaCl$. A compound has different properties than those elements that make up the compound. Elements can combine to form molecules or other compounds.

The bonds that hold these together are either covalent or ionic. In a covalent bond, atoms share electrons. In an ionic bond, atoms become ions and the atoms are held together because of the attraction of the positive and negative charges. Mixtures are combinations of substances that have not undergone a chemical change but only a physical change. Sugar water is a good example of a mixture. A solution is a mixture such as sugar water. The substance in a solution that is dissolved, the sugar in sugar water for example, is called the solute. The substance in which the solute is dissolved, the water for example, is called the solvent. Solutions can also be gases or solids. An alloy, or a mixture of two or more metals, is a solution.

Atoms, molecules, and elements form matter or anything that has weight and takes up space. An object's mass refers to the amount of matter it contains. An object's weight refers to the amount of gravitational force that is placed upon it. The mass of an object can stay constant, while an object's weight can change. For example, an astronaut may be six feet tall and may weigh 200 pounds on earth. In a space shuttle outside the earth's atmosphere, though, the astronaut still measures six feet tall but has no weight because of a lack of gravity. Generally speaking, matter has three possible states—solid, liquid, and gas. The state of matter can be changed by adding or removing energy. For example, an ice cube, a solid, can be changed to a liquid by adding heat. If heat is added to the liquid, water, the liquid becomes a gas, steam. The temperature at which a solid becomes a liquid is known as the melting point, while the temperature at which a liquid becomes a gas is known as the boiling point. The temperature at which a gas becomes a liquid is known as the condensation point, and the temperature at which a liquid becomes a solid is known as the freezing point. These changes are all physical changes.

In chemical changes, or chemical reactions, the atoms or ions of one or more substances are changed so that the result is one or more different substances. The substances that are changed are called reactants, and the resulting substances are called products.

During a chemical reaction, matter is neither created nor destroyed, so the mass of the product or products is always the same as the mass of the reactants. Chemical reactions can be written as chemical equations. In a chemical equation, the reactants are on the left side of the equation, and the products are on the right side of the equation. In a chemical equation, the total number of atoms must be the same on each side of the equation since the mass does not change. In all chemical reactions, there is a transfer of energy. An endothermic reaction is when the reactants absorb energy. An exothermic reaction is when energy is given off, often in the form of heat.

Energy can be defined as the ability to set an object in motion by applying force. Energy comes in a variety of forms. Heat and light are both very common examples of energy. Electrical energy, nuclear energy, chemical energy, and mechanical energy are also common forms of energy. The two basic types of energy are potential energy and kinetic energy. An object has potential energy when it is in a position to move. When the object moves, it has kinetic energy. For example, a bowling ball in a bowler's hand has potential energy, but a bowling ball rolling toward the pins has kinetic energy. When the ball hits the pins, energy is transferred. The transfer of energy can be measured in joules. The ball that hit the pins was obviously in motion, but all objects are in motion even when they seem to be at rest. Because the earth is rotating, all objects are in motion. There are three important concepts to remember when talking about motion. Speed is the rate at which an object moves, velocity is an object's speed in a particular direction, and acceleration is the rate at which the velocity changes. There are also several important laws that apply to motion. The law of inertia says that an object at rest will stay at rest until a force acts upon it. The law also says that an object in motion will stay in motion in a straight line at a constant speed until a force acts upon it. The law of constant acceleration says that if a constant force is applied to an object, the object will move with constant acceleration in the direction of the force. The law of conservation of momentum says that for every action, there is an equal and opposite reaction.

One of the most practical and commonly used forms of energy is electricity. Electricity is based on the movement of charged particles. This movement of charged particles is called an electric current. Battery-operated devices use direct current or a current that flows in one direction only. Appliances and other things that are "plugged in" use alternating current or a current that flows back and forth. An object or substance, such as metal, that allows an electrical current to flow through it is called a conductor. A substance that does not allow the flow of an electrical current is called an insulator. Glass and rubber are both good insulators. As an electric current flows through a conductor, it creates a magnetic field. This magnetic field affects magnetic substances much the may a magnet does. An electromagnet uses a coiled wire with a current running through it to create a magnetic field, while a permanent magnet uses spinning electrons to create a magnetic field. Every magnet has two poles, a north pole and a south pole. Opposite poles are attracted, while like poles repel each other. Moving magnetic fields are used to power motors and generators by creating electric currents. An electric current that is sent through a transformer can be changed into a different voltage to allow various products to harness the electrical energy.

5. PRACTICING SCIENCE QUESTIONS

Directions: Items 1 and 2 are based on the following passage.

A food web is made up of linking food chains. The two basic types of food webs are the grazing web and the detrital web. In the grazing web, the chain begins with plants that are passed to herbivores (plant eaters) and then to carnivores (flesh eaters) or omnivores (those that eat both plants and animals). For example, cows, which are herbivores, eat grass, and humans are omnivores who, in turn, might eat beef products.

The detrital web begins with plant and animal matter that become decomposers (bacteria and fungi). The decomposers then pass to detritivores (organisms that feed on decomposed matter) and then to carnivores. In this web, the decomposed matter is fed upon by earthworms for example, and some species of birds will eat the worms. The predators that feed upon birds are carnivores.

The two webs can overlap because animals could eat the plants that grow in the decomposed matter, and some animals are both plant and flesh eaters.

1. A carnivore eats
   (1) both plants and animals.
   (2) only plants.
   (3) only animals.
   (4) plants and decomposers.
   (5) plants, animals, and decomposers.

2. The main ides of this selection is
   (1) decomposed matter is eaten by omnivores.
   (2) vegetarians don't eat meat.
   (3) food webs are separate and distinct.
   (4) the detrital web overlaps into the grazing web.
   (5) animals only fit into the grazing web.

Directions: Items 3 and 4 refer to the following passage:

Erosion is the process by which rock and soil is moved on the surface of the earth, generally by a natural process. There are five basic ways that erosion can take place. Weathering takes place when the climate of an area affects the land. Hot or cold weather can expand or contract rocks and minerals, causing erosion. Rainy weather can have the effect of leeching the soil of minerals, causing erosion. Wind erosion, especially in arid climates, causes particles of soil and sand to be moved. Sand dunes are caused by the wind blowing. Glacial erosion occurs over a long period of time and removes rocks as the glacier melts. Coastal erosion occurs because of the action of the waves of the oceans and is particularly severe during storms. Water erosion occurs when the ground is saturated with moisture. Excess water runs off, carrying with it loose soil.

3. One can infer from the passage that erosion in the Sahara desert is most likely the result of
   (1) wind erosion.
   (2) weathering.
   (3) coastal erosion.
   (4) water erosion.
   (5) glacial erosion.

4. Hurricanes in Florida can, over a period of time, change the shape of its beaches. This is a result of
   (1) water erosion.
   (2) coastal erosion.
   (3) weathering.
   (4) wind erosion.
   (5) glacial erosion.

Directions: Items 5 and 6 refer to the following passage.

The ocean is constantly moving, although in the greatest depths the movement is extremely slow. This movement continually provides oxygen to the water. The surface currents that move the water are caused by prevailing winds, which in turn are related to the density of the water that varies according to temperature and salinity. Heating at the equator causes the water to become less dense, while the opposite occurs at the poles through cooling.

5. It was once thought that dangerous radioactive waste could be sealed in a container and dropped to the bottom of the ocean. This would destroy the ecology of the ocean by
   (1) taking up valuable space that should be preserved for marine animals.
   (2) allowing the waste to mix with the oxygen in the water.
   (3) ruining the bottom of the ocean.
   (4) affecting the surface currents.
   (5) causing a difference in the temperature of the ocean.

6. A high rate of evaporation in the Mediterranean Sea increases the salinity of the water. In turn,
   (1) there is less oxygen in the water.
   (2) there are fewer prevailing winds over the Mediterranean Sea.
   (3) the currents move more slowly.
   (4) the water is warmer.
   (5) the water is more dense.

Answer Explanations

1. **The correct answer is (3).** Carnivores eat only meat.

2. **The correct answer is (4).** Food chains link to form webs; decomposed matter, which is made up of plant and animal matter, is consumed by herbivores; and they in turn can be consumed by carnivores, which results in an overlapping of food webs.

3. **The correct answer is (1).** The only possible way that the Sahara would suffer erosion is from the wind.

4. **The correct answer is (2).** Hurricanes hit the coast with such great force that they can actually shape the beaches of Florida.

5. **The correct answer is (2).** If the container developed a leak, the waste would leak out and mix with the water's oxygen and spread as a result of the ocean currents.

6. **The correct answer is (5).** The water becomes more dense because evaporation leaves less water with the same amount of saline.

Day 14

Preparing for Language Arts, Reading

Topics for today:

1. Introduction to the Language Arts, Reading Test

2. Fiction on the Language Arts, Reading Test

3. Poetry on the Language Arts, Reading Test

4. Drama on the Language Arts, Reading Test

5. Business-Related Documents on the Language Arts, Reading Test

6. Commentary on the Language Arts, Reading Test

7. Practicing Language Arts, Reading Questions

1. INTRODUCTION TO THE LANGUAGE ARTS, READING TEST

The Language Arts, Reading Test contains 40 questions that you will have 65 minutes to answer. The questions will be based on a variety of reading passages that range up to 400 words in length. The reading passages will include works of fiction, one poem, one piece of drama, and some nonfiction. The nonfiction will include one business-related document and at least one article or editorial concerning art or some other visual representation. There will be no visuals on the Language Arts, Reading Test. Of the reading passages on the test, 75 percent will be literary and 25 percent will be nonfiction. This means that 30 questions will be based on fiction, poetry, and drama, while 10 questions will be based on the remaining reading passages. Approximately 20 percent of the questions will require comprehension skills, 15 percent application skills, 30–35 percent analysis skills, and 30–35 percent synthesis skills.

2. FICTION ON THE LANGUAGE ARTS, READING TEST

Works of fiction are simply written works that are made up or created by the author and do not claim to be completely true or factual. Fiction can be in the form of a short story, novel, poem, or drama. In this section, we'll examine the fiction in the form of a short story or novel excerpt. The Language Arts, Reading Test will measure your ability to use comprehension, application, analysis, and synthesis skills to understand works of fiction. In other words, you will be reading works of fiction in order to find the main idea of the passages, find and examine details, and make inferences. On Day 8, you learned about the fundamental elements of fiction such as plot, setting, and the person in which fiction can be written. With that information in mind, let's look at what you can expect to see in the reading passages and the questions.

The passages of fiction on the Language Arts, Reading Test may be from one of any number of time periods, including both classical and contemporary. In addition, the passages may be from a variety of authors, with each having a different ethnicity, age, and purpose for writing. The passages will vary so that the test can measure your ability to comprehend information within a variety of contexts. Most of the passages will be up to 400 words in length. To give you an idea of how long that is, the text you have read thus far in Day 14 is around 400 words in length. That should give you an idea of how long it may take to read 400 words of text. Keep in mind, though, that you will be reading the passages looking for things like the main idea along with details about the characters, setting, or mood. A 400-word passage is a very manageable piece of text; you should have little difficulty reading 400 words and remembering the information within the text. Before you read the passages, you may want to skim over the questions so that you have an idea about what clues or information you should be looking for as you read the passage. Also, as you read the passage, you may want to underline parts of the passage that relate to the questions that you skimmed over before you began reading. As you read the fiction, remember that the questions will not ask you to identify some obscure, hidden meaning of the passage. Rather, the questions will require you to find the main idea, identify the tone, put items in a correct sequence, or predict a character's future action based on what you read. As long as you are familiar with the terms most often used with fiction and as long as you read the passage intent on finding the main idea, mood, setting, and traits of the characters, you will be successful with the questions relating to the works of fiction.

3. POETRY ON THE LANGUAGE ARTS, READING TEST

The Language Arts, Reading Test will contain one poem that will be between 8 and 25 lines in length. As with the fiction passage, a poem of this length is very manageable. There is really no limit as to the type of poem that you will see. It may be a contemporary poem by a female author or it may be a classical poem by a classical poet. Regardless of the type of poem you encounter, the guidelines for reading and understanding it remain the same. On Day 8, you learned about the verbal tools that poets often use to create visual images or tell stories through poetry. Therefore, you already have a good idea of how to read and understand poetry. With that information in mind, glance at the questions before you read the poem so you know if you should be watching for symbolism, personification, or some other figurative language within the poem. Also, read the title of the poem and, after you have read the poem, think about how the title relates to the poem itself. As you read the poem, you may try this helpful technique. To the side of the poem, rewrite the lines or stanzas in your own words so that you can refer back to your own summary of the poem when answering the questions. In addition, this helpful hint may help you organize your thoughts about the poem. Also, you may want to underline any examples of personification, alliteration, etc. within the lines of the poem so that you can quickly locate the examples if you need to refer to the poem. As with the fiction, the poetry selection will not contain an obscure double meaning or an extremely vague main idea. By using the information both from this section and from Day 8, you will be able to successfully read and understand the poem on the test and answer the questions that accompany the poem.

4. DRAMA ON THE LANGUAGE ARTS, READING TEST

The Language Arts, Reading Test will contain one piece of drama. Although there is no line limit or word limit for the drama, you can expect the reading passage to be a reasonable length, comparable to the other reading passages on the test. As with the poem, the drama may be from one of any number of playwrights and time periods. Also like the poem, the same rules for understanding drama apply, regardless of the playwright or the time period in which it was written. On Day 8, you learned how drama is organized and how to understand drama. Use that information as you read the drama. Browse the questions before you read the passage to get an idea of what to focus on while you read the passage. Also, try to get a visual image in your mind of the story that is being told in the reading passage. Pay close attention to the stage directions because they will help you visualize how and where the story of the drama is unfolding. Take note of the way the characters speak and act toward one another. The questions may require you to identify the relationship between particular characters. The questions relating to the drama may also require you to summarize the scene, identify the setting, place the scene in a greater context, or make some other inferences from the passage. The questions will not require you to have knowledge of other parts of the drama, but you may be required to predict the future actions of the characters based on the passage. In addition, the questions will not require you to identify details about the drama as minute as details within an excerpt of a novel or short story.

5. BUSINESS-RELATED DOCUMENTS ON THE LANGUAGE ARTS, READING TEST

The Language Arts, Reading Test will contain one business-related document. This document, which will be up to 400 words in length, may be a memo, an excerpt of a training manual, a business letter, or some other text that might be found in a business setting. The test will measure your ability to read a business communication and understand the point or purpose of the document. In a practical, real-world setting, a business communication is intended to give instructions, convey important information, or raise employee awareness concerning a particular issue. A misunderstanding of a business communication could have serious consequences in the business world. The business-related document on the test will be very similar to a real business communication. Therefore, the questions relating to the document will require you to comprehend the overall meaning of the document and to make inferences that an employee might be required to make. Before you read the document, survey the questions so that you know what to look for as you read. Next, consider the title or subject of the document; this should give you a clue as to the meaning or the context of the document. As you read the document, consider both the author and the audience. Also, consider the tone of the document. These clues will help you be successful with the questions relating to the document.

6. COMMENTARY ON THE LANGUAGE ARTS, READING TEST

The Language Arts, Reading Test will include a reading passage that is a commentary or critique of another written work, a play or production, or even a work of art. If the commentary concerns a written work or a play, it will likely contain some description of the work. If the commentary concerns a work of art, it will likely contain a visual description of the art. As you read the commentary, try to imagine the story, the production, or the artwork. The questions may require you to draw conclusions based upon the description. The commentary will be written, of course, from a particular point of view based on the author's opinion. Being a work based on opinion, the commentary must not be mistaken for fact. The questions relating to the commentary will measure your ability to make inferences about the thing that the author has critiqued. The questions will also measure your ability to distinguish between fact and opinion. Keep these in mind as you read the commentary and answer the questions and you will be successful with the commentary on the test.

7. Practicing Language Arts, Reading Questions

Directions: Item 1 refers to the following document, an excerpt from **Moby Dick** *by Herman Melville.*

Call me Ishmael. Some years ago—never mind how long precisely—having little or no money in my purse, and nothing particular to interest me on shore, I thought I would sail about a little and see the watery part of the world. It is a way I have of driving off the spleen, and regulating the circulation. Whenever I find myself growing grim about the mouth; whenever it is a damp, drizzly November in my soul; whenever I find myself involuntarily pausing before coffin warehouses, and bringing up the rear of every funeral I meet; and especially whenever my hypos get such an upper hand of me, that it requires a strong moral principle to prevent me from deliberately stepping into the street, and methodically knocking people's hats off—then, I account it high time to get to sea as soon as I can.

1. The author of the passage compares the sea to which of the following?

    (1) A coffin

    (2) Therapeutic treatment for physical and emotional maladies

    (3) A funeral procession

    (4) A watery world

    (5) A ship

Directions: Item 2 refers to the following document.

Sonnet To Liberty by Oscar Wilde

Not that I love thy children, whose dull eyes
See nothing save their own unlovely woe,
Whose minds know nothing, nothing care to know,—
But that the roar of thy Democracies,

Thy reigns of Terror, thy great Anarchies,
Mirror my wildest passions like the sea
And give my rage a brother —! Liberty!
For this sake only do thy dissonant cries
Delight my discreet soul, else might all kings
By bloody knout or treacherous cannonades
Rob nations of their rights inviolate
And I remain unmoved—and yet, and yet,
These Christs that die upon the barricades,
God knows it I am with them, in some things.

2. In the passage above, the line " These Christs that die upon the barricades," is used as a metaphor for which of the following?

    (1) The author's children

    (2) The author's brother

    (3) Democracies

    (4) Liberty

    (5) Soldiers who died for liberty

Directions: Item 3 refers to the following document, an excerpt from Henrik Ibsen's, "An Enemy of the People."

Dr. Stockmann. Yes, yes, I see well enough; the whole lot of them in the town are cowards; not a man among them dares do anything for fear of the others. (Throws the letter on to the table.) But it doesn't matter to us, Katherine. We are going to sail away to the New World, and—

Mrs. Stockmann. But, Thomas, are you sure we are well advised to take this step?

Dr. Stockmann. Are you suggesting that I should stay here, where they have pilloried me as an enemy of the people—branded me—broken my windows! And just look here, Katherine—they have torn a great rent in my black trousers too!

Mrs. Stockmann. Oh, dear!—and they are the best pair you have got!

Dr. Stockmann. You should never wear your best trousers when you go out to fight for freedom and truth. It is not that I care so much about the trousers, you know; you can always sew them up again for me. But that the common herd should dare to make this attack on me, as if they were my equals—that is what I cannot, for the life of me, swallow!

Mrs. Stockmann. There is no doubt they have behaved very ill toward you, Thomas; but is that sufficient reason for our leaving our native country for good and all?

Dr. Stockmann. If we went to another town, do you suppose we should not find the common people just as insolent as they are here? Depend upon it, there is not much to choose between them. Oh, well, let the curs snap—that is not the worst part of it. The worst is that, from one end of this country to the other, every man is the slave of his Party. Although, as far as that goes, I daresay it is not much better in the free West either; the compact majority, and liberal public opinion, and all that infernal old bag of tricks are probably rampant there too. But there things are done on a larger scale, you see. They may kill you, but they won't put you to death by slow torture. They don't squeeze a free man's soul in a vice, as they do here. And, if need be, one can live in solitude. (Walks up and down.) If only I knew where there was a virgin forest or a small South Sea island for sale, cheap—

Mrs. Stockmann. But think of the boys, Thomas!

Dr. Stockmann (standing still). What a strange woman you are, Katherine! Would you prefer to have the boys grow up in a society like this? You saw for yourself last night that half the population are out of their minds; and if the other half have not lost their senses, it is because they are mere brutes, with no sense to lose.

Mrs. Stockmann. But, Thomas dear, the imprudent things you said had something to do with it, you know.

3. Which of the following is the best summary for the above passage?

   (1) A husband and wife are considering moving out of town because they are not getting along with the citizens there.

   (2) A husband and wife have been declared Public Enemy #1.

   (3) A husband wants to leave his family and live in a forest.

   (4) A man is upset because he ripped his pants.

   (5) A man wants to go exploring in the New World with his wife.

Directions: Item 4 refers to the following document.

The J.C. Smith Museum yesterday opened its latest exhibit, Art of the Midwest. The oil paintings of the exhibit showed little creativity and inspired but a yawn. The colors blended together like the shades of brown in a Midwestern corn field in the midst of a drought. The sketches resembled those of my 11-year-old nephew in his fifth-grade art class. The sculptures displayed in the museum showed some promise and potential. However, they lack the excellent vision necessary to highlight a major exhibition. The one bright spot of the show was the exquisite watercolors of Midwestern farm scenes. The watercolors portrayed the everyday life on Midwestern farms with the grandeur of the great artists or our time.

4. Which of the following can be said safely regarding the exhibit?

   (1) The author of the commentary dislikes the Midwest.

   (2) The art at the exhibit was bad art.

   (3) The art at the exhibit was good art.

   (4) The author of the commentary disliked most of the art at the exhibit.

   (5) The author of the commentary disliked all of the art at the exhibit.

Directions: Item 5 refers to the following document.

Woodbury School Faculty Handbook

Section 4 Paragraph 3—Faculty Tutoring Students for Compensation

It is the policy of the Woodbury School that full-time and part-time faculty members be prohibited from tutoring Woodbury School students either during or after school hours. It is the belief of the Woodbury School that such tutoring would create a conflict of interest for the faculty member who would tutor. Woodbury School students should have ample opportunity for instruction and tutoring by Woodbury School faculty outside the classroom at no charge or fee in addition to the Woodbury School tuition. Instances of such tutoring shall warrant suspension or dismissal of the faculty member who collects pay for tutoring Woodbury School students.

5. Based on the passage above, which of the following might also be prohibited in the faculty handbook?

    (1) A faculty member using a student as a babysitter

    (2) A faculty member buying raffle tickets from a student

    (3) A coach instructing an athlete for pay during the summer

    (4) A faculty member conducting a free exam review session after school hours

    (5) A faculty member hiring a student to cut the lawn

Answer Explanations

1. **The correct answer is (2).** The author says that he heads for the sea when he is feeling bad, emotionally and physically, because the sea makes him feel better.

2. **The correct answer is (5).** The "Christs" are the soldiers who died to save liberty.

3. **The correct answer is (1).** The husband and wife are discouraged because the citizens of the town in which they live are harassing them. Therefore, they are considering leaving.

4. **The correct answer is (4).** The author speaks unfavorably about all of the art except for the watercolors.

5. **The correct answer is (3).** Like a teacher tutoring a student for pay in an academic field, a coach working with an athlete for pay would also be prohibited.

Day 15

Preparing for Mathematics

Topics for today:

1. Introduction to the Mathematics Test
2. Strategies for the Mathematics Test
3. Important Formulas and Equations for the Mathematics Test

1. INTRODUCTION TO THE MATHEMATICS TEST

The GED Mathematics Test actually contains two parts, or booklets. Each booklet contains 25 questions, and you will have 90 minutes to answer the 50 mathematics questions. On the first 25 questions, you will be allowed to use a calculator. The calculator you will use is the Casio fx-260 solar calculator. We will examine that calculator closely in Day 16. On the second 25 questions, the use of a calculator is not permitted. Most of the questions on the Mathematics Test are multiple choice. A few questions, though, require you to mark the correct answer in an answer grid or on a plane. We will look at those questions in Day 16, too. Of the total number of mathematics questions, 25 percent of the questions will measure skills in numbers, number sense, and operations; 25 percent of the questions will measure skills in data, statistics, and probability; 25 percent of the questions will measure skills in algebra; and 25

percent of the questions will measure skills in geometry. The majority of the questions on the Mathematics Test can be answered using reasoning skills and basic addition, subtraction, multiplication, division, and basic algebra and geometry. Many of the questions will be presented as word problems, or practical everyday situations. If you are worried about remembering all the formulas from algebra and geometry, you will delighted to know that you will be given a sheet that contains many important formulas. You may use these formulas on the test.

The two chapters in this book about the Mathematics Test will focus on strategies for the mathematics and instructions for the calculator and the alternate format questions. For a complete review of the content of the Mathematics Test, you should consult the book *Master the GED—Mathematics*, also by ARCO. It contains step-by-step instructions for solving each type of mathematics question you might see on the GED as well as two full-length practice tests with detailed answer explanations.

2. STRATEGIES FOR THE MATHEMATICS TEST

The first and most important thing to remember when taking the GED Mathematics Test is to read every question and answer choice carefully before you begin the calculations. After you carefully read the question and the answers, you should determine whether or not you know how to work the problem. If you do, solve the problem as quickly as you can without rushing, and make sure your answer is one of the possible answer choices. If it is, mark the correct answer and move to the next problem. However, if you do not know how to solve the problem, you should follow these steps. First, make sure you know what the question is asking. When you determine what the question is asking, try to develop an equation that will help you solve any unknowns in the problem. If you can develop a formula, plug each of the answer choices into the equation. When an answer choice does not work in the equation, eliminate that answer choice. When an answer choice works in the equation, go with that answer choice. By following these hints, you can attack problems you know how to solve and save time for those that may be more difficult for you.

As you read through the answer choices, beware of answer choices that simply repeat numbers that are presented in the problem, especially if the problem is a word problem. Many times, incorrect answer choices are simply numbers from the problem either repeated or written in some form or variation. If the problem is difficult, answer choices like these are most probably incorrect.

When you are working with word problems, you can save yourself some time by estimating and rounding numbers in the problem. For example, if you are working with the number 63, ask yourself if 63 is closer to 60 or 70. Since 63 is closer to 60, you can substitute 60 for 63 and probably do the math in your head. When you get your answer, see if it is close to one of the answer choices. You can also use the same method by rounding to the nearest hundred and nearest thousand.

As you have already learned, you should carefully read each of the answer choices before you begin work on the problem. Another important reason for carefully reading each answer choice is to make sure you are working in the same format as the answer choices. For example, if the problem is worded so that you have to calculate meters but the answer choices are all written in kilometers, you should make your calculations in kilometers.

An important point to remember is that there is no penalty for a wrong answer. With this in mind, you should not spend too much time on any one question. Rather than spending your minutes working to answer a difficult question, you could probably answer 2 or 3 other questions in the same amount of time. Therefore, use your time to answer all the questions that are not difficult for you first and then move on to the others. Your score will be much better if you answer all the easier ones correctly and some of the more challenging ones correctly than if you answer only a few of each correctly. Also, remember to monitor your time so that just before time expires, you can quickly answer any questions you have not had time to work on.

You will be provided with scratch paper before the test, and you should use the scratch paper every chance you get. If it helps you to rewrite or rephrase a question, do so on the scratch paper. If you need to draw a picture or a diagram to help you visualize what a question is asking, do so on the scratch paper. If you need to remember a formula, a theorem, a postulate, or an equation that is not provided for you, jot it down on the scratch paper as soon as you get it. You may also use the scratch paper for additional calculations. Don't be surprised when the test moderator asks to collect the scratch paper after the test. The testing service is not going to grade your scratch work or anything else you have on your scratch paper. In addition, nothing on your scratch paper will have any effect on your test score. The testing service collects the scratch paper so that test takers cannot write down the test problems and then take them away from the testing center.

The last, and one of the most important, tips you should use is this: if you have extra time at the end of the test, go back and check your work. The most common mistakes that are made on math tests result from careless mistakes and not a lack of knowledge of mathematics. These careless mistakes often happen when test takers try to rush through the test in order to finish in a given amount of time. By going back over your work and checking for mistakes, you may discover some of these mistakes and raise your score in the process.

3. IMPORTANT FORMULAS AND EQUATIONS FOR THE MATHEMATICS TEST

Geometry

To find the perimeter of a triangle: $P = a+b+c$

To find the perimeter of a square: $P = 4s$

To find the area of a triangle: $A = \frac{1}{2}bh$

To find the area of a square: $A = s^2$

To find the area of a rectangle: $A = lw$

To find the area of a parallelogram: $A = bh$

To find the area of a trapezoid: $A = \frac{1}{2}h(b_1 + b_2)$

The Pythagorean Theorem: $a^2 + b^2 = c^2$

To find the circumference of a circle: $C = \pi d$

To find the area of a circle: $A = \pi r^2$

To find the volume of a cube: $V = s^3$

To find the volume of a rectangular solid: $V = lwh$

To find the volume of a cylinder: $V = \pi r^2 h$

Algebra

The order of operations is as follows:

1. operations inside parentheses
2. operations with square roots and exponents
3. multiplication and division
4. addition and subtraction

The distributive law: $a(b+c) = ab+ac$

The associative law: $(a+b)+c = a+(b+c)$

The commutative law: $a+b = c$ is the same as $b+a = c$

Day 16

Using the Calculator and the Alternate Format Answer Grid on the Mathematics Test

Topics for today:

1. Using the Calculator on the Mathematics Test
2. Practicing with the Calculator
3. Using the Alternate Format Answer Grid on the Mathematics Test
4. Tips to Remember when using the Calculator and the Alternate Format Grid on the Mathematics Test

1. USING THE CALCULATOR ON THE MATHEMATICS TEST

When you take the GED Mathematics Test, you will be allowed to use a calculator on part of the test and not on the other part of the test. You will not be allowed to bring and use your own calculator. Instead, you will be provided with a Casio fx-260 solar calculator at the testing center. Even though you will be provided with instructions on how to use the calculator, it would probably be a good idea for you to purchase the Casio fx-260 solar calculator at an office supply store to practice with before the test. Let's take a look at the calculator you will be using on the test.

Casio fx-260 Solar Calculator

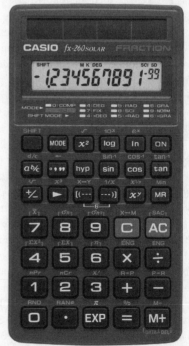

Casio is a registered trademark of Casio Computer Co. Ltd. Used with permission of Casio.

Although you will be allowed to use the calculator on the first part of the test, you are not required to use the calculator on all the questions. You should use the calculator to help with long or complicated functions or sets of numbers. Let's turn on the calculator and try a few problems.

To turn on the calculator, press the **ON** key in the upper right hand corner. Let's try the following problem: 54+26+199+32+13=? To solve this problem press the following keys in this order: **5 4 + 2 6 + 1 9 9 + 3 2 + 1 3 =** and the answer on the display should be **324**. Let's try another: 97+22–46+123–86+5–12=? Before you work another problem, press the **AC** key to clear all previous calculations. To solve this problem, press the following keys in this order: **9 7 + 2 2 – 4 6 + 1 2 3 – 8 6 + 5 – 1 2 =** and the answer on the display should be **103**. Now let's try some multiplication and division problems. Use your calculator to solve this problem: 46995 ÷ 65=? To solve this problem press the **AC** key and then the following keys in this order: **4 6 9 9 5 ÷ 6 5 =** and the answer on the display should be **723**. Now let's try another: 758×9=? To solve this problem, press the **AC** key then the following keys in this order: **7 5 8 × 9 =** and the answer on the display should be **6822**. If you need to solve a problem with a decimal point, simply insert the decimal point after the appropriate number by pressing the **.** key. Let's look at an example: 4.5–2.66=? To solve this problem, press the **AC** key then press the following keys in this order: **4 . 5 – 2 . 6 6 =** and the answer on the display should be **1.84**.

Now let's do some calculations that involve a few more steps. If you look at the keys on the calculator, you will notice yellow symbols and functions above the keys. To use these functions, you must press the **SHIFT** key, found in the upper left hand corner, then the key below the function you want to use. For example, if you want to use the % key, you should press the **SHIFT** key and then press the **=** key. Let's try a few problems that will require you to use the **SHIFT** key. Use your calculator to solve this problem: 30% of 1850 = ? To solve this problem, press the **AC** key then the following keys in this order: **1 8 5 0 × 3 0 SHIFT =** and the answer on the display should be **555**. Let's try this problem: Find the square root of 1369. To find

the answer to this problem, press the **AC** key then the following keys in this order: **1 3 6 9 SHIFT** x^2 and the answer on the display should be **37**.

Now let's look at a problem that involve the use of parentheses. If you have a problem such as 10(42 ÷ 6), then you simply need to press the keys as you see the problem written. Use your calculator to solve the problem above. To solve the problem, press the **AC** key then press the following keys in this order: **1 0 (4 2 ÷ 6) =** and the answer on the display should be **70**.

Another important function that your calculator can do is changing the sign of a number. Many problems on the GED may require you to add positive and negative numbers, so you will need to change signs of numbers using your calculator. Let's look at the problem −12 − −6 =? Use your calculator to solve the problem. To solve the problem, press the **AC** key then press the following keys in this order: **1 2 +/– − 6 +/– =** and the answer on the display should be **–6**.

2. PRACTICING WITH THE CALCULATOR

Use the instructions above to use your calculator to answer the following practice questions. After you answer the questions, check your answers with the answer explanations.

1. 435+62+98=

2. 23.9–14.4=

3. $72 \times 3 \times 16 =$

4. 90% of 18770 is ?

5. The square root of 144 is ?

6. –27 – 17 – –4 =

7. 32–9+14–12+67=

8. 10π=

9. 12(9+3+5-2)=

10. 42.7– –12.1=

Answer Explanations

1. $4\ 3\ 5 + 6\ 2 + 9\ 8 =$ and the answer is **595**
2. $2\ 3\ .\ 9 - 1\ 4\ .\ 4 =$ and the answer is **9.5**
3. $7\ 2 \times 3 \times 1\ 6 =$ and the answer is **3456**
4. $1\ 8\ 7\ 7\ 0 \times 9\ 0$ **SHIFT** $=$ and the answer is **16893**
5. $1\ 4\ 4$ **SHIFT** x^2 and the answer is **12**
6. $2\ 7 +/- -1\ 7 - 4 +/- =$ and the answer is **–40**
7. $3\ 2 - 9 + 1\ 4 - 1\ 2 + 6\ 7 =$ and the answer is **92**
8. $1\ 0 \times$ **SHIFT EXP** and the answer is **31.415926535**
9. $1\ 2\ (\ 9 + 3 + 5 - 2\ ) =$ and the answer is **180**
10. $4\ 2\ .\ 7 - 1\ 2\ .\ 1 +/- =$ and the answer is **54.8**

---

3. USING THE ALTERNATE FORMAT ANSWER GRID ON THE MATHEMATICS TEST

Of the 50 questions you will see on the GED Mathematics Test, approximately 10 questions will not be multiple choice. These questions are called Alternate Format questions. Instead of choosing the correct answer from a list of answer choices, you will need to color in circles on an answer grid like the one below.

Other alternate format questions, perhaps only 1 or 2, will require you to plot a point on a graph such as the one below.

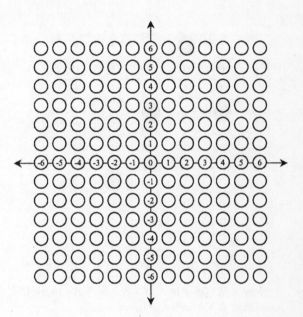

Let's take a look at how to use the answer grid to mark your answer. Let's use the problem 3–.75=? as our problem. The correct answer is 2.25. To record this answer in an answer grid, you would write the answer across the top of the grid with one number or sign in each column. In the first column you would write **2**, in the second column you would write **.**, in the third column you would write **2,** and in the fourth column you would write **5**. Next, you would completely color in the corresponding number or sign in the column below each number or sign. For example, in the first column you would color in the **2**, in the second column you would color in the **.**, and so on. Using the answer grid is that simple. A completed answer grid for the above problem would look like this:

2	.	2	5	
	(/)	(/)	(/)	
(•)	●	(•)	(•)	(•)
(0)	(0)	(0)	(0)	(0)
(1)	(1)	(1)	(1)	(1)
●	(2)	●	(2)	(2)
(3)	(3)	(3)	(3)	(3)
(4)	(4)	(4)	(4)	(4)
(5)	(5)	(5)	●	(5)
(6)	(6)	(6)	(6)	(6)
(7)	(7)	(7)	(7)	(7)
(8)	(8)	(8)	(8)	(8)
(9)	(9)	(9)	(9)	(9)

Now let's take a look at a graph. Let's mark the coordinate (2,–3) on the graph below.

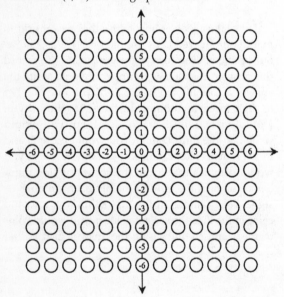

The first number is on the x-axis, which means that the point will be either to the right or left of the y-axis. The second number is on the y-axis, which means that the point will be either above or below the x-axis. The first number in our coordinate is 2, so you should move two places along the x-axis to the right. The second number is –3, so you should move down 3 spaces from the point you just marked. Color in that circle. Your graph should look like the one below.

4. TIPS TO REMEMBER WHEN USING THE CALCULATOR AND THE ALTERNATE FORMAT GRID ON THE MATHEMATICS TEST

When using the calculator, always clear the display by using the **AC** key before working the next problem.

When you work problems with the calculator, make sure the answer seems reasonable. If the calculator gives you an answer that seems unreasonable, you may have pressed a wrong key during your calculations.

Be careful with every keystroke on the calculator to avoid careless mistakes.

Don't forget to use the **SHIFT** key to use the second functions on your calculator.

When filling in the answer grids and graphs, take your time to avoid careless mistakes.

You may begin in any column on the answer grid, as long as you leave yourself room to fit the entire answer in the grid.

On the graphs, run your pencil along the circles to make sure that you are straight both vertically and horizontally when you graph coordinates.

Day 17

Test-Taking Strategies

Topic for today:

1. Test-Taking Strategies for the GED Candidate

1. TEST-TAKING STRATEGIES FOR THE GED CANDIDATE

Of course there is no substitute for preparation and knowledge of the test material when it comes to taking the GED Tests. However, there are a few general tips, hints, and strategies you should be familiar with before you begin the practice tests. While you take the practice tests, use these strategies. By practicing these strategies on the practice tests, you will be even more prepared for success on the actual GED Tests. Let's look at some of the most important strategies to use on the GED Tests:

1. **Read each question carefully and make sure you know what the question is asking.** Look for clue words such as *evaluate, main idea, analyze, true,* or *valid.* These words can be clues about how to answer the question. On mathematics questions, make sure you see all the mathematical signs and that you know exactly what functions you need to perform to answer the question.

2. **Choose an answer that answers the question being asked.** This may seem obvious, but you should be careful not to choose an answer that doesn't even fit the question. For example, don't select an answer choice if it gives supporting facts when the question asks for the main idea. This is especially important on the Science, Social Studies, and Language Arts, Reading Tests.

3. **When answering multiple-choice questions, try to eliminate as many incorrect answers as possible.** If you can eliminate 2 or 3 incorrect answer choices on a question you may not know, your odds of guessing the correct answer more than double. Once you eliminate an incorrect answer choice, mark through it so you don't come back to it by mistake.

4. **When reading through text on a reading passage item, underline or circle the main idea of each paragraph.** This will help you remember the main idea and will help you locate the main idea again if you have to refer to the paragraph later.

This is especially important on the Social Studies, Science, and Language Arts, Reading Tests.

5. **When using graphics in visual items, be sure to read the title or caption that may accompany the map, chart, graph, picture, or cartoon.** Many times, the title or caption will give you a clue about the true meaning of the visual. You can then use this clue to help clarify the question and eliminate incorrect answers.

6. **Use common sense.** Some questions may be unfamiliar to you at first glance. However, you use and make decisions every day about things with which you are not very familiar. Use your real-life, practical problem-solving skills and good old-fashioned common sense to help you on the test.

7. **If you don't know the answer, guess!** Because there is no penalty for guessing on the GED Tests, you should never leave a question unanswered. If you don't know the answer, guess. If you are almost out of time and have several left, go through them and guess. You have nothing to lose and everything to gain by leaving no question unanswered.

8. **Don't try to cram all the GED Tests in a short period of time.** You won't be taking these tests in one sitting, and you won't be required to take them all in one week. Spread them out so that you allow yourself plenty of time to prepare adequately for each one.

9. **Make sure you are well rested and well fed before you take the test.** In order for your mind to be its sharpest, you should feel fresh and not tired. Also make sure that you eat before you take the GED Tests. Like your body, your brain needs energy, too!

10. **Relax and be confident in your abilities!** Don't be nervous about taking the GED Tests. These tests are practical measures of knowledge that you have gained not only through study but also through life experiences. The test is not designed to trick you or cause frustration. Therefore, find confidence and reassurance in the hard work and hours of preparation you have invested in this endeavor and do great job!

Day 18

Review Before You Begin the Practice Tests

Topics for today:

1. Review the content areas in which you feel the least confident
2. Review the content areas in which you feel the most confident

1. REVIEW THE CONTENT AREAS IN WHICH YOU FEEL THE LEAST CONFIDENT

Before you begin the practice tests, take a few minutes to skim over the two areas in which you feel the least confident. If math has never been your strength, use your time today to review the math chapters. If writing is where you feel you need the most improvement, spend your time reviewing the writing skills chapters. If you need to reread a chapter or two, that is fine. If you feel good about all the areas, just skim through the chapters. After you review, go back over the practice questions in the chapters your reviewed. Read the questions and the answer explanations. This last little review before the practice tests may help information stick with you, and it may refresh your memory on a few important points. When you are ready, move on to the areas in which you feel the most comfortable.

2. REVIEW THE CONTENT AREAS IN WHICH YOU FEEL THE MOST CONFIDENT

Take just a few minutes and skim through the chapters that cover the content areas in which you feel the most confident and comfortable. Use this time as a quick review. Refresh your memory about exactly what will be tested and reinforce the information that you already know. After you have skimmed the chapters, do the practice questions and read the answer explanations. This will further reinforce your confidence in these areas. When you finish this review, resist the temptation to start the next chapter. After you have studied, do something relaxing and fun. You shouldn't cram right before the tests. You have put in your time studying and preparing, and you will be ready for the practice tests that begin tomorrow. You just might surprise yourself about how much you will remember tomorrow from today's study session. Go on, put the book down and come back tomorrow for your first practice test!

Day 19 to Day 28

The Practice Tests

Day 19

Language Arts, Writing Practice Test (Part I)

Directions

The following directions are reprinted with the permission of the GED Testing Service.

The Language Arts, Writing Test measures your ability to use clear and effective English. It is a test of English as it should be written, not as it might be spoken. This test includes both multiple-choice questions and essay. The following directions apply only to the multiple-choice section; a separate set of directions is given for the essay.

The multiple-choice section consists of paragraphs with numbered sentences. Some of the sentences contain an error in sentence structure, usage, or mechanics (punctuation and capitalization). After reading the numbered sentences, answer the multiple-choice questions that follow. Some questions refer to sentences that are correct as written. The best answer for these questions is the one that leaves the sentence as originally written. The best answer for some questions is the one that produces a sentence that is consistent with the verb tense and point of view used throughout the text.

You will have 2 hours to complete this test. Spend no more than 75 minutes on the 50 multiple-choice questions, leaving the remaining time for the essay. Work carefully, but do not spend too much time on any one question. Answer every question. You may begin working on the essay section of this test as soon as you complete the multiple-choice section.

Do not mark in this test booklet. Record your answers on the separate answer sheet provided. Be sure that all requested information is properly recorded on the answer sheet.

To record your answers, fill in the numbered circle on the answer sheet that corresponds to the answer you select for each question in the test booklet.

EXAMPLE:

Sentence 1: **We were all honored to meet governor Phillips and his staff.**

What correction should be made to sentence 1?

    (1) Change <u>were</u> to <u>was</u>

    (2) Insert a comma after <u>honored</u>

    (3) Change <u>governor</u> to <u>Governor</u>

    (4) Insert a comma after <u>Phillips</u>

    (5) No correction is necessary

In this example, the word *governor* should be capitalized; therefore, answer space (3) would be marked on the answer sheet.

Do not rest the point of your pencil on the answer sheet while you are considering your answer. Make no stray or unnecessary marks. If you change an answer, erase your first mark completely. Mark only one answer space for each question; multiple answers will be scored as incorrect. Do not fold or crease your answer sheet. All test materials must be returned to the test administrator.

Directions: Choose the one best answer to each item. Items 1 to 8 refer to the following paragraph.

(1)These days, more and more people are choosing to spend there vacations at home. (2)Some people choose to stay home since they are afraid to travel by plane. (3)Others choose to stay home because they do not want to spend for an expensive trip. (4)Often, the reason for staying home is to spend quiet time with family. (5)The important thing about a vacation is that they are used in a way enjoyable to the person taking it. (6)The goal is to feel refreshed and rejuvenated upon returning to work. (7)For some, the excitement of traveling is outweighed by the exhaustion they feel after the trip is over. (8)One person must determine how best he or she can benefit from vacation time.

1. Sentence 1: These days, more and more people are choosing to spend there vacations at home.

   What correction should be made to this sentence?

   (1) Change <u>people</u> to <u>persons</u>
   (2) Change <u>there</u> to <u>their</u>
   (3) Change <u>at</u> to <u>in</u>
   (4) Change <u>days</u> to <u>day</u>
   (5) No correction is necessary

2. Sentence 2: Some people choose to stay home since they are afraid to travel by plane.

   What correction should be made to this sentence?

   (1) Change <u>since</u> to <u>because</u>
   (2) Change <u>Some</u> to <u>More</u>
   (3) Change <u>stay home</u> to <u>stay at home</u>
   (4) Change <u>travel by plane</u> to <u>travel with a plane</u>
   (5) No correction is necessary

3. Sentence 3: Others choose to stay home because they do not want to spend for an expensive trip.

   What correction should be made to this sentence?

   (1) Change <u>because</u> to <u>since</u>
   (2) Add <u>that costs a lot</u> to the end of the sentence
   (3) Change <u>spend</u> to <u>pay</u>
   (4) Change <u>choose</u> to <u>chose</u>
   (5) No correction is necessary

4. Sentences 4 and 5: Often, the reason for staying home is to spend quiet time <u>with family. The</u> important thing about a vacation is that they are used in a way enjoyable to the person taking it.

   Which of the following is the best way to write the underlined portion of the two sentences?

   (1) with family. The
   (2) with family, the
   (3) with family and the
   (4) with family; the
   (5) with family; and the

5. Sentence 5: The important thing about a vacation is that they are used in a way enjoyable to the person taking it.

   What correction should be made to this sentence?

   (1) Change <u>thing</u> to <u>thought</u>
   (2) Change <u>vacation</u> to <u>vacationing</u>
   (3) Change <u>they are</u> to <u>it is</u>
   (4) Change <u>it</u> to <u>them</u>
   (5) No correction is necessary

6. Sentence 6: The goal is to feel refreshed and rejuvenated upon returning to work.

   What correction should be made to this sentence?

   (1) Place a colon after refreshed
   (2) Change <u>upon</u> to <u>for</u>
   (3) Change <u>returning</u> to <u>returns</u>
   (4) Change <u>The</u> to <u>A</u>
   (5) No correction is necessary

7. Sentence 7: For some, the excitement of traveling is outweighed by the exhaustion they feel after the trip is over.

   What correction should be made to this sentence?

   (1) Change <u>For</u> to <u>In</u>
   (2) Replace the comma after <u>some</u> to a semicolon
   (3) Change <u>after</u> to <u>when</u>
   (4) Change <u>exhaustion</u> to <u>exhausting</u>
   (5) No correction is necessary

8. Sentence 8: One person must determine how best he or she can benefit from vacation time.

   What correction should be made to this sentence?

   (1) Change <u>One</u> to <u>Each</u>
   (2) Change <u>he or she</u> to <u>they</u>
   (3) Change <u>benefit</u> to <u>benefits</u>
   (4) Change <u>time</u> to <u>thyme</u>
   (5) No correction is necessary

Directions: Items 9 to 17 refer to the following two paragraphs:

(1)Fannie Flagg wrote this novel, "Fried Green Tomatoes at the Whistle Stop Cafe." (2)She wrote it during the 1980s, and places the story partially in a modern-day nursing home. (3)However, she also tells of rural Alabama during the first half of the century. (4)The story is moving and inspiring. (5)The novel was too popular that it was made into a major motion picture. (6)It is not uncommon for popular books to be made into a movie. (7)Some of the best movies originated from written works and not as scripts for a movie. (8)This does not just refer to novels. (9)Lots of Shakespeare's plays have been made into popular movies. (10)"Romeo and Juliet," "Hamlet," and "Macbeth." (11)It is good that books can be made into movies. (12)Otherwise, many people would never no of those inspirational works of literature.

9. Sentence 1: Fannie Flagg wrote this novel, "Fried Green Tomatoes at the Whistle Stop Cafe."

   What correction should be made to this sentence?

   (1) Change <u>wrote</u> to <u>written</u>
   (2) Change <u>Cafe."</u> to <u>Cafe".</u>
   (3) Take out the quotation marks
   (4) Change <u>this novel</u> to <u>the novel</u>
   (5) No correction is necessary

10. Sentence 2: She wrote it during the 1980s, and places the story partially in a modern-day nursing home.

    What correction should be made to this sentence?

    (1) Change <u>it</u> to <u>of it</u>
    (2) Change <u>1980s</u> to <u>1980-s</u>
    (3) Change <u>places</u> to <u>placed</u>
    (4) Change <u>partially</u> to <u>partly</u>
    (5) No correction is necessary

11. Sentence 3: However, she also tells of rural Alabama during the first half of the century.

    What correction should be made to this sentence?

    (1) Change <u>However</u> to <u>For example</u>
    (2) Change <u>half</u> to <u>have</u>
    (3) Remove the comma
    (4) Change <u>half</u> to <u>1/2</u>
    (5) No correction is necessary

12. Sentence 5: The novel was too popular that it was made into a major motion picture.

    What correction should be made to this sentence?

    (1) Change <u>made</u> to <u>created</u>
    (2) Change <u>picture</u> to <u>pitcher</u>
    (3) Change <u>too</u> to <u>so</u>
    (4) Change <u>major</u> to <u>minor</u>
    (5) No correction is necessary

13. Sentence 7: Some of the best movies originated from written works and not as scripts for a movie.

    What correction should be made to this sentence?

    (1) Change <u>a movie</u> to <u>movies</u>
    (2) Change <u>Some</u> to <u>More</u>
    (3) Change <u>originated</u> to <u>started</u>
    (4) Change <u>from written</u> to <u>from the written</u>
    (5) No correction is necessary

14. Sentence 9: Lots of Shakespeare's plays have been made into popular movies.

    What correction should be made to this sentence?

    (1) Change <u>Shakespeare's</u> to <u>Shakespeares</u>
    (2) Change <u>have been</u> to <u>has been</u>
    (3) Change <u>Lots</u> to <u>Many</u>
    (4) Change <u>made</u> to <u>maid</u>
    (5) No correction is necessary

15. Sentences 9 and 10: Lots of Shakespeare's plays have been made into popular <u>movies. "Romeo</u> and Juliet," "Hamlet," and "Macbeth".

    Which of the following is the best way to write the underlined portion of the two sentences?

    (1) movies. "Romeo
    (2) movies, "Romeo
    (3) movies, including "Romeo
    (4) movies; "Romeo
    (5) movies: "Romeo

16. Sentence 10: "Romeo and Juliet," "Hamlet," and "Macbeth".

    What correction should be made to this sentence?

    (1) Remove the quotation marks after Juliet
    (2) Remove the quotation marks after Hamlet
    (3) Remove the quotation marks after Macbeth
    (4) Change <u>"Macbeth".</u> to <u>"Macbeth."</u>
    (5) No correction is necessary

17. Sentence 12: Otherwise, many people would never no of those inspirational works of literature.

    What correction should be made to this sentence?

    (1) Change <u>Otherwise</u> to <u>However</u>
    (2) Change <u>many</u> to <u>lots</u>
    (3) Change <u>those</u> to <u>them</u>
    (4) Change <u>no</u> to <u>know</u>
    (5) No correction is necessary

Directions: Items 18 to 24 refer to the following paragraph.

(1)I don't hardly ever get to visit my best friend. (2)I really like going to visit her often. (3)Its always fun when we spend time together. (4)Me and her always go to the beach. (5)We where bathing suits and swim in the ocean. (6)Sometimes we see fish in the see. (7)I wish I was at the beach now.

18. Sentence 1: I don't hardly ever get to visit my best friend.

    What correction should be made to this sentence?

    (1) Change <u>don't</u> to <u>do not</u>
    (2) Delete <u>don't</u>
    (3) Delete <u>hardly</u>
    (4) Change <u>best friend</u> to <u>bestfriend</u>
    (5) No correction is necessary

19. Sentence 2: I really like going to visit her often.

    What correction should be made to this sentence?

    (1) Delete <u>going</u>
    (2) Change <u>to</u> to <u>too</u>
    (3) Delete <u>often</u>
    (4) Change <u>really</u> to <u>sure</u>
    (5) No correction is necessary

20. Sentence 3: Its always fun when we spend time together.

    What correction should be made to this sentence?

    (1) Change <u>Its</u> to <u>It's</u>
    (2) Replace <u>always</u> with <u>all ways</u>
    (3) Change <u>when</u> to <u>win</u>
    (4) Change the period to an exclamation mark
    (5) No correction is necessary

21. Sentence 4: Me and her always go to the beach.

    What correction should be made to this sentence?

    (1) Change <u>Me and her</u> to <u>She and me</u>
    (2) Change <u>Me and her</u> to <u>She and I</u>
    (3) Change <u>Me and her</u> to <u>I and her</u>
    (4) Change <u>Me and her</u> to <u>I and she</u>
    (5) No correction is necessary

22. Sentence 5: We where bathing suits and swim in the ocean.

    What correction should be made to this sentence?

    (1) Change <u>where</u> to <u>wear</u>
    (2) Change <u>where</u> to <u>were</u>
    (3) Change <u>bathing suits</u> to <u>bathingsuits</u>
    (4) Change <u>swim</u> to <u>swam</u>
    (5) No correction is necessary

23. Sentence 6: Sometimes we see fish in the see.

    What correction should be made to this sentence?

    (1) Change the first <u>see</u> to <u>sea</u>
    (2) Change <u>Sometimes</u> to <u>Some times</u>
    (3) Change the second <u>see</u> to <u>sea</u>
    (4) Change <u>fish</u> to <u>fishes</u>
    (5) No correction is necessary

24. Sentence 7: I wish I was at the beach now.

    What correction should be made to this sentence?

    (1) End the sentence with a question mark
    (2) Change <u>was</u> to <u>were</u>
    (3) Change <u>now</u> to <u>know</u>
    (4) Replace the second <u>I</u> with <u>we</u>
    (5) No correction is necessary

Directions: Items 25 to 31 refer to the following paragraph.

(1)Preparing for a party is all ways a hard thing to do. (2)If you clean your house a head of time, it makes it easier. (3)You have to plan because you do not want the party to be boaring. (4)I have been too many parties where I was bored. (5)A good party has got to have music and food. (6)If you make these selections in advance, you're guests are sure to have a good time. (7)If they have a good time, they'll probably come back, next year.

25. Sentence 1: Preparing for a party is all ways a hard thing to do.

    What correction should be made to this sentence?

    (1) Change <u>is</u> to <u>as</u>
    (2) Change <u>all ways</u> to <u>always</u>
    (3) Put a semicolon after <u>party</u>
    (4) Change <u>to</u> to <u>too</u>
    (5) No correction is necessary

26. Sentence 2: If you clean your house a head of time, it makes it easier.

    What correction should be made to this sentence?

    (1) Replace <u>your</u> with <u>you are</u>
    (2) Replace <u>your</u> with <u>you're</u>
    (3) Change <u>a head</u> to <u>ahead</u>
    (4) Replace <u>If</u> with <u>Since</u>
    (5) No correction is necessary

27. Sentence 3: You have to plan because you do not want the party to be boaring.

    What correction should be made to this sentence?

    (1) Replace <u>because</u> with <u>since</u>
    (2) Change the second <u>you</u> to <u>You</u>
    (3) End the sentence with an exclamation mark
    (4) Change <u>boaring</u> to <u>boring</u>
    (5) No correction is necessary

28. Sentence 4: I have been to too many parties where I was bored.

    What correction should be made to this sentence?

    (1) Change <u>too</u> to <u>to</u>
    (2) Change <u>have</u> to <u>had</u>
    (3) Replace <u>where</u> with <u>wear</u>
    (4) Replace <u>bored</u> with <u>board</u>
    (5) No correction is necessary

29. Sentence 5: A good party has got to have music and food.

    What correction should be made to this sentence?

    (1) Insert <u>have</u> before <u>food</u>
    (2) Change <u>got</u> to <u>gotta</u>
    (3) Change <u>has got to</u> to <u>must</u>
    (4) Insert a colon after <u>have</u>
    (5) No correction is necessary

30. Sentence 6: If you make these selections in advance, you're guests are sure to have a good time.

    What correction should be made to this sentence?

    (1) Replace <u>these</u> with <u>this</u>
    (2) Change <u>you're</u> to <u>your</u>
    (3) Change <u>you're</u> to <u>you are</u>
    (4) Replace <u>If</u> with <u>Where</u>
    (5) No correction is necessary

31. Sentence 7: If they have a good time, they'll probably come back, next year.

    What correction should be made to this sentence?

    (1) Change <u>they'll</u> with <u>they will</u>
    (2) Insert <u>the</u> before <u>next</u>
    (3) Delete <u>probably</u>
    (4) Delete the second comma
    (5) No correction is necessary

Directions: Items 32 to 41 refer to the following document.

ACME E-MAIL POLICY

PURPOSE: (1)This policy provides guidelines for using of ACME's electronic mail (e-mail) system. (2)It applies to all e-mail sent or received by em-ployees of ACME employment. (3)These guidelines don't supercede any state or federal laws, or any other ACME policies regarding confidentiality, information dissemination, or standards of conduct.

GUIDELINES:

1. Business Use. (4)ACME's e-mail system is only property of ACME. (5)Use of the e-mail system, accept in the limited circumstances listed below, is for official ACME business only. (6)Access to e-mail is a privilege, and not a right. (7)The privilege may be revoked at any time, for any reason or without the necessity for stating a reason.

2. Confidentiality. (8)Employees should not have no expectation of privacy regarding their use of the e-mail system and e-mail content. (9)All e-mail is subject to inspection and audit by management, or its representatives, at any time, with or with out notice. (10)By using ACME's e-mail system, an employee agrees that ACME has a right to inspect and audit all e-mail communications, and consents to any inspections following proper procedures and protocols as to be determined by management.

32. Sentence 1: This policy provides guidelines for using of ACME's electronic mail (e- mail) system.

    What correction should be made to this sentence?

    (1) Change <u>provides</u> to <u>provide</u>
    (2) Replace <u>using</u> with <u>use</u>
    (3) Change <u>guidelines</u> to <u>guideline's</u>
    (4) Replace <u>for</u> with <u>to</u>
    (5) No correction is necessary

33. Sentence 2: It applies to all e-mail sent or received by employees of ACME employment.

    What correction should be made to this sentence?

    (1) Replace <u>received</u> with <u>receive</u>
    (2) Change <u>employees</u> to <u>employed</u>
    (3) Delete <u>employment</u>
    (4) Change <u>employment</u> to <u>employees</u>
    (5) No correction is necessary

34. Sentence 3: These guidelines don't supercede any state or federal laws, or any other ACME policies regarding confidentiality, information dissemination, or standards of conduct.

    What correction should be made to this sentence?

    (1) Replace <u>don't</u> with <u>do not</u>

    (2) Delete the first comma

    (3) Delete the last comma

    (4) Replace <u>These</u> with <u>This</u>

    (5) No correction is necessary

35. Sentence 4: ACME's e-mail system is only property of ACME.

    What correction should be made to this sentence?

    (1) Insert <u>the</u> before <u>only</u>

    (2) Insert <u>the</u> after <u>only</u>

    (3) Replace <u>only property</u> with <u>property only</u>

    (4) Delete <u>only</u>

    (5) No correction is necessary

36. Sentence 5: Use of the e-mail system, accept in the limited circumstances listed below, is for official ACME business only.

    What correction should be made to this sentence?

    (1) Replace <u>Use</u> with <u>Using</u>

    (2) Replace <u>accept</u> with <u>except</u>

    (3) Insert a comma after <u>accept</u>

    (4) Change <u>in</u> to <u>for</u>

    (5) Delete only

37. Sentence 6: Access to e-mail is a privilege, and not a right.

    What correction should be made to this sentence?

    (1) Change <u>Access</u> to <u>Excess</u>

    (2) Replace <u>to</u> with <u>two</u>

    (3) Delete <u>and</u>

    (4) Delete the comma and <u>and</u>

    (5) No correction is necessary

38. Sentence 7: The privilege may be revoked at any time, for any reason or without the necessity for stating a reason.

    What correction should be made to this sentence?

    (1) Replace <u>may</u> with <u>shall</u>

    (2) Add a comma after <u>reason</u>

    (3) Change <u>without</u> to <u>with out</u>

    (4) Change <u>a reason</u> to <u>the reason</u>

    (5) No correction is necessary

39. Sentence 8: Employees should not have no expectation of privacy regarding their use of the e-mail system and e-mail content.

    What correction should be made to this sentence?

    (1) Delete <u>not</u>

    (2) Delete <u>no</u>

    (3) Replace <u>their</u> with <u>there</u>

    (4) Change <u>should not</u> to <u>shouldn't</u>

    (5) No correction is necessary

40. Sentence 9: All e-mail is subject to inspection and audit by management, or its representatives, at any time, with or with out notice.

    What correction should be made to this sentence?

    (1) Replace <u>All</u> with <u>Any</u>

    (2) Replace <u>its</u> with <u>it's</u>

    (3) Change <u>with out</u> to <u>without</u>

    (4) Change <u>any</u> to <u>all</u>

    (5) No correction is necessary

41. Sentence 10: By using ACME's e-mail system, an employee agrees that ACME has a right to inspect and audit all e-mail communications, and consents to any inspections following proper procedures and protocols as to be determined by management.

    What correction should be made to this sentence?

    (1) Replace <u>using</u> with <u>use of</u>

    (2) Replace <u>has</u> with <u>had</u>

    (3) Change <u>procedures</u> to <u>procedure</u>

    (4) Delete <u>to be</u>

    (5) No correction is necessary

Directions: Items 42 to 50 refer to the following document.

(1)In 1962, the Soviet Union begin building missile sites in Cuba. (2)In secret. (3)An American spy plane discovers the Cuban missile sites in October of that same year. (4)President Kennedy decided that the missiles posed a threat to the security of the United States so he ordered the Soviet's to remove the missiles. (5)Kennedy then used American ships to quarantine the island nation of Cuba so no more ships with missiles could reach Cuba. (6)American troops gathered in Florida in case they needed to in vade Cuba. (7)The Soviets, did not want to, back down. (8)The whole world feared the two countries would launch a nuclear attack on one each other. (9) Eventually, the Soviets removed the missiles and nuclear war was avoided.

42. Sentence 1: In 1962, the Soviet Union begin building missile sites in Cuba.

    What correction can be made?

    (1) Change <u>begin</u> to <u>began</u>
    (2) Change <u>begin</u> to <u>beginning</u>
    (3) Change <u>building</u> to <u>built</u>
    (4) Change <u>in</u> to <u>under</u>
    (5) No correction is necessary

43. Sentence 2: In secret.

    What correction can be made?

    (1) Change <u>secret</u> to <u>secretly</u>
    (2) Delete <u>In secret</u> and add <u>in secret</u> to Sentence 1
    (3) Change <u>In secret</u> to <u>In complete secrecy</u>
    (4) Change <u>In secret</u> to <u>Secretly</u>
    (5) No correction is necessary

44. Sentence 3: An American spy plane discovers the Cuban missile sites in October of that same year.

    What correction can be made?

    (1) Change <u>American spy</u> to <u>American, spy</u>
    (2) Change <u>in October of that</u> to <u>in October, of that</u>
    (3) Change <u>discovers</u> to <u>discovered</u>
    (4) Change <u>spy plane</u> to <u>spy-plane</u>
    (5) No change is necessary

45. Sentence 4: President Kennedy decided that the missiles posed a threat to the security of the United States so he ordered the Soviet's to remove the missiles.

    What correction can be made?

    (1) Change <u>Soviet's</u> to <u>Soviets</u>
    (2) Change <u>President Kennedy decided</u> to <u>President Kennedy, decided</u>
    (3) Change <u>so he ordered</u> to <u>so he orders</u>
    (4) Change <u>that the missiles</u> to <u>because the missiles</u>
    (5) No correction is necessary

46. Sentence 5: Kennedy then used American ships to quarantine the island nation of Cuba so no more ships with missiles could reach Cuba.

    What correction can be made?

    (1) Change <u>Kennedy then used American ships to</u> to <u>Kennedy, then used American ships, to</u>
    (2) Change <u>then</u> to <u>than</u>
    (3) Change <u>no</u> to <u>know</u>
    (4) Change <u>quarantine</u> to <u>quarrel</u>
    (5) No change is necessary

47. Sentence 6: American troops gathered in Florida in case they needed to in vade Cuba.

    What correction can be made?

    (1) Change <u>they</u> to <u>Kennedy</u>
    (2) Change <u>in vade</u> to <u>invade</u>
    (3) Change <u>American</u> to <u>American's</u>
    (4) Change <u>troops</u> to <u>troop's</u>
    (5) No change is necessary

48. Sentence 7: The Soviets, did not want to, back down.

    What correction can be made?

    (1) Change <u>Soviets</u> to <u>Soviet's</u>
    (2) Delete <u>to</u>
    (3) Delete both commas
    (4) Change <u>did not</u> to <u>didn't</u>
    (5) No correction is necessary

49. Sentence 8: The whole world feared the two countries would launch a nuclear attack on one each other.

    What correction can be made?

    (1) Change <u>whole</u> to <u>hole</u>
    (2) Change <u>two</u> to <u>too</u>
    (3) Change <u>each other</u> to <u>another</u>
    (4) Change <u>nuclear</u> to <u>nuke</u>
    (5) No change is necessary

50. Sentence 9: Eventually, the Soviets removed the missiles and nuclear war was avoided.

    What correction can be made?

    (1) Change <u>nuclear war was avoided</u> to <u>avoided nuclear war</u>
    (2) Change <u>Soviets</u> to <u>Soviet's</u>
    (3) Change <u>Soviets removed</u> to <u>Soviets, removed</u>
    (4) Change <u>removed</u> to <u>remained</u>
    (5) No change is necessary

Answer Explanations

1. **The correct answer is (2).** The word <u>their</u> is correct, and the word <u>there</u> is the homonym of <u>their</u>.

2. **The correct answer is (1).** The correct word to use here is <u>because</u>.

3. **The correct answer is (3).** The correct word to use here is <u>pay</u>.

4. **The correct answer is (4).** A semicolon is a good way to make the transition between the two independent clauses.

5. **The correct answer is (3).** The pronoun and verb must agree with the word <u>vacation</u>.

6. **The correct answer is (5).** This sentence is correct and needs no correction.

7. **The correct answer is (3).** The correct word to use here is <u>when</u>.

8. **The correct answer is (1).** The correct word to use is <u>Each</u> instead of <u>One</u>.

9. **The correct answer is (4).** The correct word to use is <u>the</u> instead of <u>this</u>.

10. **The correct answer is (3).** The word <u>placed</u> agrees with the verb <u>wrote</u>.

11. **The correct answer is (5).** No correction is necessary in this sentence.

12. **The correct answer is (3).** The correct word to modify popular is <u>so</u>.

13. **The correct answer is (1).** The word <u>movies</u> should agree with <u>scripts</u>.

14. **The correct answer is (3).** <u>Lots</u> is much weaker language than <u>many</u>.

15. **The correct answer is (3).** The sentence fragment can be added to the first sentence by replacing the period with a comma.

16. **The correct answer is (4).** The quotation marks should be placed outside the period.

17. **The correct answer is (4).** The word <u>no</u> should be replaced its homonym <u>know</u>.

18. **The correct answer is (2).** The word <u>don't</u> is unnecessary and weakens the sentence.

19. **The correct answer is (1).** In this sentence, the word <u>going</u> used with <u>to visit</u> is poor grammar.

20. **The correct answer is (1).** <u>It's</u> is the contraction for <u>It is</u>.

21. **The correct answer is (2).** The compound subject of the sentence should be in subjective case instead of objective case.

22. **The correct answer is (1).** The correct word to use is the verb <u>wear</u> instead of its homonym <u>where</u>.

23. **The correct answer is (3).** The correct word is <u>sea</u> instead of its homonym <u>see</u>.

24. **The correct answer is (2).** The correct tense of the verb is <u>were</u> instead of <u>was</u>.

25. **The correct answer is (2).** The correct word is <u>always</u> instead of the two words <u>all ways</u>.

26. **The correct answer is (3).** The two words <u>a head</u> should be replaced with <u>ahead</u>.

27. **The correct answer is (4).** The word <u>boring</u> is the correct word to use in this sentence.

28. **The correct answer is (1).** The word <u>too</u> should be replaced with its homonym <u>to</u>.

29. **The correct answer is (3).** The phrase <u>has got to</u> is language that weakens the sentence.

30. **The correct answer is (2).** The contraction <u>you're</u> should be replaced with the possessive <u>your</u>.

31. **The correct answer is (4).** The second comma is not needed and should be deleted.

32. **The correct answer is (2).** The word <u>using</u> should be replaced with the word <u>use</u>.

33. **The correct answer is (3).** The word <u>employment</u> is redundant and should be deleted.

34. **The correct answer is (5).** No correction is necessary in this sentence.

35. **The correct answer is (4).** The word <u>only</u> weakens the sentence and should be deleted.

36. **The correct answer is (2).** The correct word is <u>except</u> instead of its homonym <u>accept,</u> which is a verb.

37. **The correct answer is (4).** The use of the commas and the word <u>and</u> weakens the sentence.

38. **The correct answer is (2).** The additional comma will clarify and reduce confusion.

39. **The correct answer is (1).** The word <u>not</u> should be deleted to avoid a double negative.

40. **The correct answer is (3).** The words <u>with out</u> should be replaced with <u>without</u>.

41. **The correct answer is (4).** The words <u>to be</u> should be deleted.

42. **The correct answer is (1).** The word <u>begin</u> should be changed to the past tense <u>began</u>.

43. **The correct answer is (2).** To avoid a sentence fragment, delete <u>In secret.</u> and add <u>in secret</u> to the previous sentence.

44. **The correct answer is (3).** The word <u>discovers</u> should be replaced by the past tense verb <u>discovered</u>.

45. **The correct answer is (1).** The possessive <u>Soviet's</u> should be replaced with the plural <u>Soviets</u>.

46. **The correct answer is (5).** No correction is necessary in this sentence.

47. **The correct answer is (2).** The words <u>in vade</u> should be changed to <u>invade</u>.

48. **The correct answer is (3).** The commas should be deleted to avoid confusion.

49. **The correct answer is (3).** The words <u>each other</u> should be changed to <u>another</u>.

50. **The correct answer is (1).** The verb should be in active voice instead of in passive voice.

Day 20

Language Arts, Writing Practice Test (Part II)

Directions

This part of the Writing Skills Test is intended to determine how well you write. You are asked to write an essay that explains something or presents an opinion on an issue. In preparing your essay, you should take the following steps.

1. Read carefully the directions and the essay topic given below.

2. Plan your essay carefully before you write.

3. Use scratch paper to make any notes.

4. Write your essay on the lined pages of the separate answer sheet.

5. Read carefully what you have written and make any changes that will improve your essay.

6. Check your paragraphs, sentence structure, spelling, punctuation, capitalization, and usage and make any necessary corrections.

Be sure you write the letter of the essay topic (given below) on your answer sheet. Write the letter in the box at the upper right-hand corner of the page where you write your essay.

You will have 45 minutes to write on the topic below. Write legibly and use a ballpoint pen so that the evaluators will be able to read your writing.

Write your essay on the lined pages of the separate answer sheet. The notes you make on scratch paper will not be scored.

Your essay will be scored by at least two trained evaluators who will judge it according to its *overall effectiveness*. They will judge how clearly you make the main point of your composition, how thoroughly you support your ideas, and how clearly and correctly you write throughout the essay.

Topic B

In light of the last presidential election, the issue of voting has been a subject of much debate.

How important is it for citizens to vote in national elections? Should people be required to vote?

Should there be requirements for voters? Does every vote really count? Respond to this statement in an essay of approximately 250 words.

Answer Explanation

As with the essay on the GED Language Arts, Writing Test, there is no right or wrong answer. The important things to check in your essay are the following:

1. Is your essay written in the five-paragraph format?

2. Is the main idea of the essay included in the first paragraph?

3. Does each paragraph that follows include information that supports the main idea?

4. Does each paragraph that follows include a topic sentence?

5. Does the final paragraph include a conclusion?

6. Does the essay stay on point and not ramble?

7. Does your essay include good grammar and good spelling?

If you can answer yes to these questions, your essay is exactly what the evaluators will be looking for in an essay.

Day 21

Social Studies Practice Test (Part I)

For the purposes of this book, the Social Studies Test will be divided into two parts so that you will have time today and tomorrow to answer questions and review the answers in the amount of time you have allotted for GED preparation. For this practice test, give yourself 32 minutes to complete all the questions for Day 21. The GED Social Studies Test will contain 50 questions.

Directions

The following are test directions reprinted by permission of the GED Testing Service.

The Social Studies Test consists of multiple-choice questions that measure general social studies concepts. The questions are based on short readings that often include a map, graph, chart, cartoon, or figure. Study the information given and then answer the question(s) following it. Refer to the information as often as necessary in answering the questions.

You will have 70 minutes to answer the 50 questions in this booklet. Work carefully, but do not spend too much time on any one question. Answer every question.

Do not mark in this answer booklet. Record your answers on the separate answer sheet provided. Be sure that all requested information is properly recorded on the answer sheet.

To record your answers, fill in the numbered circle on the answer sheet that corresponds to the answer you select for each question in this booklet.

FOR EXAMPLE:

Early colonists of North America looked for settlement sites with adequate water supplies and access by ship. For this reason, many early towns were built near

(1) mountains.

(2) prairies.

(3) rivers.

(4) glaciers.

(5) plateaus.

The correct answer is rivers; therefore, answer space (3) would be marked on the answer sheet.

Do not rest the point of your pencil on the answer sheet while you are considering your answer. Make no stray or unnecessary marks. If you change an answer, erase your first mark completely. Mark only one answer space for each question; multiple answers will be scored as incorrect. Do not fold or crease your answer sheet. All test materials must be returned to the test administrator.

Directions: Items 1 to 3 are based on the following excerpt from the Declaration of Independence.

We hold these truths to be self-evident, that all men are created equal, that they are endowed by their Creator with certain unalienable Rights, that among these are Life, Liberty and the pursuit of Happiness.—That to secure these rights, Governments are instituted among Men, deriving their just powers from the consent of the governed, — That whenever any Form of Government becomes destructive of these ends, it is the Right of the People to alter or to abolish it, and to institute new Government, laying its foundation on such principles and organizing its powers in such form, as to them shall seem most likely to effect their Safety and Happiness. Prudence, indeed, will dictate that Governments long established should not be changed for light and transient causes; and accordingly all experience hath shown, that mankind are more disposed to suffer, while evils are sufferable, than to right themselves by abolishing the forms to which they are accustomed. But when a long train of abuses and usurpations, pursuing invariably the same Object evinces a design to reduce them under absolute Despotism, it is their right, it is their duty, to throw off such Government, and to provide new Guards for their future security.—Such has been the patient sufferance of these Colonies; and such is now the necessity which constrains them to alter their former Systems of Government. The history of the present King of Great Britain is a history of repeated injuries and usurpations, all having in direct object the establishment of an absolute Tyranny over these States. To prove this, let Facts be submitted to a candid world.

1. In the passage above, which of the following is the best meaning of the line "Governments are instituted among Men, deriving their just powers from the consent of the governed?"

    (1) Those who are governed must have the consent of the government.

    (2) Those who are governed must grant the government the power to rule.

    (3) Governments are institutions of only men.

    (4) Governments do not have to have consent for their unjust powers.

    (5) Governments derive their powers from men and not women.

2. In the passage above, the word *despotism* means which of the following?

    (1) A monarchy

    (2) An anarchy

    (3) A democracy

    (4) An oligarchy

    (5) A tyrannical government

3. The document above was a precursor to which of the following armed conflicts?

    (1) The War for American Independence

    (2) The War of 1812

    (3) The U.S. Civil War

    (4) The French and Indian War

    (5) World War I

Directions: Items 4 to 6 are based on the following passage.

The Acme DVD Company is a small DVD manufacturing operation. The small company has five employees that produce 250 DVDs every day. The initial response by consumers is overwhelming and Acme cannot produce enough DVDs to keep the product available for consumers. Acme hires an extra employee to help produce more DVDs. The six employees produce only 280 DVDs each day and the down time for the employees increases. The company expands it work week from five days to seven days. After two weeks, Acme has many extra DVDs.

4. By hiring more employees and expanding its work week, Acme is responding to which of the following?

   (1) Fiscal policy

   (2) Supply

   (3) Demand

   (4) Law of diminishing returns

   (5) Macroeconomics

5. Which of the following is most likely to happen after Acme's two weeks of production with an extra employee and an expanded work week?

   (1) The price of DVDs will increase

   (2) The demand for DVDs will increase

   (3) The supply of DVDs will decrease

   (4) The price of DVDs will decrease

   (5) The price of DVDs will remain the same

6. Which of the following explains why the production of DVDs did not increase in proportion to the amount that labor increased?

   (1) The law of supply and demand

   (2) The law of deficit spending

   (3) Ohm's law

   (4) Macroeconomics

   (5) The law of diminishing returns

Directions: Items 7 and 8 are based on the following passage.

The governments of both the United States and Canada were designed so that the three branches of government were assigned three important roles. One branch of government is responsible for making the laws. One branch of government is responsible for enforcing the laws. One branch of government is responsible for interpreting the laws. These branches are the legislative branch, the executive branch, and the judicial branch, respectively.

7. The passage above describes which of the following?

   (1) Checks and balances

   (2) Federalism

   (3) Sovereignty

   (4) Separation of powers

   (5) Cooperativism

8. A similar plan for government described in the passage would most likely be found in which of the following documents?

   (1) The Constitution

   (2) The Declaration of Independence

   (3) The Federalist Papers

   (4) U.S. Supreme Court Case Roe v. Wade

   (5) U.S. Supreme Court Case Plessy v. Ferguson

Directions: Items 9 and 10 are based on the following passage.

During times of depression, a government may choose to stimulate the economy with one of any number of ways. For example, a government may create jobs to reduce unemployment. In addition, a government may lower taxes to encourage spending.

9. The passage above is an example of which of the following?

    (1) Supply and demand

    (2) Monetary policy

    (3) Fiscal policy

    (4) Inflation and recession

    (5) Taxational policy

10. The idea of spending money to get out of a depression was pioneered by which of the following?

    (1) Alan Greenspan

    (2) John Maynard Keynes

    (3) Adam Smith

    (4) Ronald Reagan

    (5) Franklin D. Roosevelt

Directions: Items 11 and 12 are based on the following passage.

The area that includes part of Pakistan and part of India is known as Kashmir. This area, though divided into two countries by a political boundary, shares a common religion and a common language. Conflict between the two countries has arisen over the area.

11. To which of the following themes of geography does this passage relate?

    (1) Location

    (2) Place

    (3) Environment

    (4) Movement

    (5) Region

12. Which of the following types of maps would a geographer use to study the information presented in the passage?

    (1) A topographical map

    (2) A weather map

    (3) A globe

    (4) A physical map

    (5) A political map

Directions: Items 13 to 15 are based on the following passage.

Europeans discovered the vast wealth of fish and whales available to commercial fisherman off the coast of Labrador and in the Gulf of St. Lawrence and in the Grand Banks. Fishermen from Spain, France, England, and Portugal all took advantage of the bountiful catch found here. Eventually, the English explorer Sir Humphrey Gilbert claimed Newfoundland for England. After the Spanish and Portuguese left the area, the English settled the northern part of Newfoundland and the French settled the southernmost part. These settlers entered into a trade relationship with the natives. The bulk of the trading was done with furs, especially of beaver furs. The European demand for beaver products, particularly hats, launched an industry that remained a vital part of the economy for many years to follow.

The indigenous peoples traded with the European settlers and formed many alliances with the Europeans. Because of the large amount of territory and the relatively small number of Europeans, few conflicts emerged between Europeans and the indigenous nations they encountered. The Europeans made some attempts to Christianize the natives, but they found very little success. The greatest negative effect of the trade relationship was the spread of European diseases to the indigenous peoples. Diseases in epidemic proportions spread quickly among the natives, and the diseases wiped great numbers of natives everywhere the Europeans went. The indigenous population continued decline even into the twentieth century.

13. The passage above describes part of the history of which of the following?

    (1) North America

    (2) South America

    (3) Australia

    (4) Africa

    (5) Asia

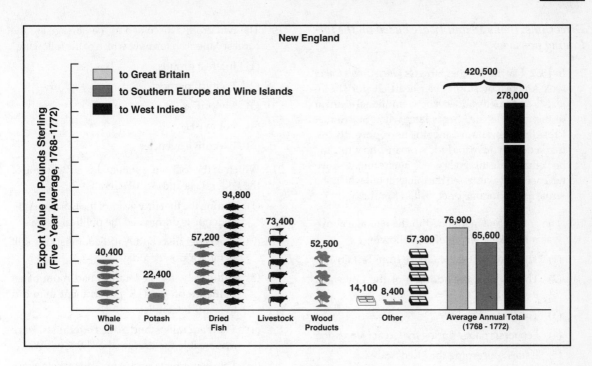

New England

Export Value in Pounds Sterling (Five-Year Average, 1768-1772)

to Great Britain
to Southern Europe and Wine Islands
to West Indies

Whale Oil	Potash	Dried Fish	Livestock	Wood Products	Other	Average Annual Total (1768 - 1772)
40,400	22,400	57,200 / 94,800	73,400	52,500	14,100 / 8,400 / 57,300	76,900 / 65,600 / 278,000 / 420,500

14. In the passage above, the word *indigenous* means which of the following?

   (1) Hostile
   (2) Diseased
   (3) Native
   (4) Non-Christian
   (5) Non-European

15. The Europeans settled in the land discussed in the passage primarily for which of the following reasons?

   (1) Religious reasons
   (2) Economic reasons
   (3) Political reasons
   (4) Social reasons
   (5) Philosophical reasons

Directions: Items 16 and 17 are based on the graph above.

16. In the years 1768–1772, imports to which of the following places accounted for the majority of the trade income of the Lower South?

   (1) The West Indies
   (2) Southern Europe
   (3) Southern Europe and the Wine Islands
   (4) Great Britain
   (5) Not enough information is given

17. Which of the following combinations of exports had the greatest value?

   (1) Corn and Other
   (2) Indigo and Naval Stores
   (3) Meat and Corn
   (4) Deerskins and Wood Products
   (5) Indigo, Deerskins, and Other

Directions: Items 18 and 19 are based on the following passage.

In 1852, Harriet Beecher Stowe's *Uncle Tom's Cabin* took America by storm. Her heartfelt story of injustice and cruelty added a new, emotional element to the great debate. Years later when Stowe met President Abraham Lincoln, he reportedly remarked, "So you're the little woman who wrote the book that made this great war." Interestingly, Stowe never actually witnessed the things about which she wrote except for one brief visit in Kentucky.

18. The *great debate* mentioned in the passage above was most likely which of the following?

    (1) The issue of independence from Britain

    (2) The issue of the addition of the Louisiana Purchase

    (3) The issue of slavery

    (4) Economic policy during the Great Depression

    (5) Issues concerning the "Red Scare"

19. The *great war* of which Lincoln spoke was which of the following?

    (1) War for American Independence

    (2) French and Indian War

    (3) Spanish American War

    (4) Korean War

    (5) U.S. Civil War

Directions: Items 20 and 21 are based on the following passage.

In the earliest days of the Republic, two ideologies dominated the political scene. One ideology, advocated by the Federalists, presented the idea that a strong central government was perhaps the proper way to design the permanent government. The other ideology, held by the Anti-Federalists, promoted a weak central government and stronger state governments. The two groups remained at political odds though in principle they wanted the same thing, a better government than the one of which they had just rid themselves.

20. The two groups discussed in the passage are the earliest American forms of which of the following?

    (1) Interest groups

    (2) Political parties

    (3) Minorities

    (4) Lobbyists

    (5) Executive agencies

21. Which of the following statements is most true of the Federalists and Anti-Federalists?

    (1) During the first fifty years of the U.S., the Anti-Federalists dominated the political scene.

    (2) The Federalists and Anti-Federalists are still vying for power today.

    (3) Ultimately, the Federalists had more of an influence on the U.S. government than did the Anti-Federalists.

    (4) The Federalists and Anti-Federalists were responsible for starting the U.S. Civil War.

    (5) The Federalists and Anti-Federalists were responsible for starting the War of 1812.

Directions: Items 22 and 23 are based on the following passage.

Latitude lines and longitude lines are imaginary lines that measure distances north and south of the equator and east and west of the equator, respectively. The farther from the equator a latitude line is, the cooler the average yearly temperature is. The closer a latitude line is to the equator, the warmer the average yearly temperature is. The latitude lines are numbered from 0° at the equator to 90° at each of the poles.

22. Which of the following conclusions can be made about latitude lines?

    (1) The average daily temperature increases as the number of the latitude line decreases.

    (2) The average daily temperature increases as the number of the latitude line increases.

    (3) The Tropics are closer to the poles than to the equator.

    (4) The lines of latitude measure east and west of the equator.

    (5) The lines of latitude can be as high as 180° because 90° + 90° = 180°.

23. Which of the following is the intersection of a latitude line and a longitude line?

    (1) A geographic location

    (2) A relative location

    (3) A point

    (4) A glyph

    (5) A coordinate

Directions: Items 24 and 25 are based on the following passage.

To the Congress of the United States:

Yesterday, Dec. 7, 1941—a date which will live in infamy—the United States of America was suddenly and deliberately attacked by naval and air forces of the Empire of Japan.

The United States was at peace with that nation and, at the solicitation of Japan, was still in conversation with the government and its emperor looking toward the maintenance of peace in the Pacific. Indeed, one hour after Japanese air squadrons had commenced bombing in Oahu, the Japanese ambassador to the United States and his colleagues delivered to the Secretary of State a formal reply to a recent American message. While this reply stated that it seemed useless to continue the existing diplomatic negotiations, it contained no threat or hint of war or armed attack. It will be recorded that the distance of Hawaii from Japan makes it obvious that the attack was deliberately planned many days or even weeks ago. During

the intervening time, the Japanese government has deliberately sought to deceive the United States by false statements and expressions of hope for continued peace.

24. In the speech above, the word *infamy* means which of the following?

    (1) Honor

    (2) Dishonor

    (3) A national museum

    (4) Mystery

    (5) Suspicion

25. Following the speech, President Roosevelt asked Congress to enter which of the following wars?

    (1) The Spanish American War

    (2) World War I

    (3) World War II

    (4) The Korean War

    (5) The Vietnam War

Answer Explanations

1. **The correct answer is (2).** The line means that a government has authority to rule because the people it governs grant the government that authority.

2. **The correct answer is (5).** The word *despotism* is used to describe an oppressive government.

3. **The correct answer is (1).** The Declaration of Independence was issued before the War for American Independence.

4. **The correct answer is (3).** The company was responding to the demand of the consumers for more DVDs.

5. **The correct answer is (4).** Because of the increase in supply, the price will most likely decrease.

6. **The correct answer is (5).** The law of diminishing returns says that there is a point where more labor does not mean more product in proportion to that labor.

7. **The correct answer is (4).** Separation of powers occurs when the three branches of government are each assigned a different responsibility or role in government.

8. **The correct answer is (1).** The Constitution is a written plan or blueprint for government.

9. **The correct answer is (3).** The passage describes a government's fiscal policy.

10. **The correct answer is (2).** The correct answer is John Maynard Keynes because he introduced the idea of spending out of depression and recession.

11. **The correct answer is (5).** The correct answer is region because the area is unified by a common language and religion.

12. **The correct answer is (5).** A political map would show the political boundaries between and around the area mentioned in the passage.

13. **The correct answer is (1).** The passage discusses Canada, which is part of North America.

14. **The correct answer is (3).** The word *indigenous* is synonymous with *native*.

15. **The correct answer is (2).** The Europeans settled in Canada for the economic benefits of the fish and furs.

16. **The correct answer is (4).** Great Britain accounted for more trade income than the West Indies and Southern Europe and Wine Islands combined.

17. **The correct answer is (3).** The largest combination is Meat and Corn.

18. **The correct answer is (3).** Harriet Beecher Stowe's book was about the cruelties of slavery.

19. **The correct answer is (5).** Lincoln, Stowe, and slavery were all contemporary with the U.S. Civil War.

20. **The correct answer is (2).** The Federalists and Anti-Federalists were political parties.

21. **The correct answer is (3).** The central government of the U.S. is based more on Federalist ideology than on Anti-Federalist ideology.

22. **The correct answer is (1).** The temperature increases closer to the equator, so the lines of latitude closest to the equator, also the lines with the lowest numbers, will run through warmer climatic conditions.

23. **The correct answer is (5).** A coordinate is the intersection of a latitude line and a longitude line.

24. **The correct answer is (2).** The word *infamy* means *dishonor*.

25. **The correct answer is (3).** After the speech, the Congress declared war on Japan and entered World War II.

Day 22

Social Studies Practice Test (Part II)

For the purposes of this book, the Social Studies Test will be divided into two parts so that you will have time today and tomorrow to answer questions and review the answers in the amount of time you have allotted for GED preparation. For this practice test, give yourself 33 minutes to complete all the questions for Day 22. The GED Social Studies Test will contain 50 questions.

Social Studies Directions

The following are test directions reprinted by permission of the GED Testing Service.

The Social Studies Test consists of multiple-choice questions intended to measure your knowledge of general social studies concepts. The questions are based on short readings that often include a graph, chart, or figure. Study the information given and then answer the question(s) following it. Refer to the information as often as necessary in answering the questions.

You should spend no more than 75 minutes answering the questions in this booklet. Work carefully, but do not spend too much time on any one question. Be sure you answer every question. You will not be penalized for incorrect answers.

Do not mark in this test booklet. Record your answers to the questions on the separate answer sheet provided. Be sure all requested information is properly recorded on the answer sheet.

To record your answers, mark the numbered space on the answer sheet beside the number that corresponds to the question in the test booklet.

FOR EXAMPLE:

Early colonists of North America looked for settlement sites that had adequate water supplies and were accessible by ship. For this reason, many early towns were built near

(1) mountains.

(2) prairies.

(3) rivers.

(4) glaciers.

(5) plateaus.

The correct answer is rivers; therefore, answer space (3) would be marked on the answer sheet.

Do not rest the point of your pencil on the answer sheet while you are considering your answer. Make no stray or unnecessary marks. If you change an answer, erase your first mark completely. Mark only one answer space for each question; multiple answers will be scored as incorrect. Do not fold or crease your answer sheet. Return all test materials to the test administrator.

Directions: Items 26 to 28 are based on the following passage.

In 2002, twelve countries introduced a new currency called the Euro. The twelve countries include Austria, Belgium, Finland, France, Germany, Greece, Ireland, Italy, Luxembourg, the Netherlands, Portugal, and Spain. The new currency will replace all the currencies formerly used by the twelve countries. Each of the countries has locked in an exchange rate for its former currency. Also, a standard interest rate has been set for borrowing the Euro. Eventually, more countries may adopt the Euro and move toward one currency.

26. The twelve countries are part of an economic group known as which of the following?

    (1) European Euro Group

    (2) NATO

    (3) OPEC

    (4) European Union

    (5) United States of Euro

27. By establishing an exchange rate and an interest rate, the governments of these countries are exercising which of the following?

    (1) Fiscal policy

    (2) Domestic policy

    (3) Monetary policy

    (4) Diplomatic policy

    (5) Taxation policy

28. The use of a single currency over an entire continent might be most accepted in countries with which of the following?

    (1) A socialist economy

    (2) A communist economy

    (3) A capitalist economy

    (4) A pure economy

    (5) A mixed economy

Directions: Items 29 to 31 are based on the following passage by John O'Sullivan.

The American people having derived their origin from many other nations, and the Declaration of National Independence being entirely based on the great principle of human equality, these facts demonstrate at once our disconnected position as regards any other nation; that we have, in reality, but little connection with the past history of any of them, and still less with all antiquity, its glories, or its crimes. On the contrary, our national birth was the beginning of a new history, the formation and progress of an untried political system, which separates us from the past and connects us with the future only; and so far as regards the entire development of the natural rights of man, in moral, political, and national life, we may confidently assume that our country is destined to be the great nation of futurity.

America is destined for better deeds. It is our unparalleled glory that we have no reminiscences of battle fields, but in defense of humanity, of the oppressed of all nations, of the rights of conscience, the rights of personal enfranchisement. Our annals describe no scenes of horrid carnage, where men were led on by hundreds of thousands to slay one another, dupes and victims to emperors, kings, nobles, demons in the human form called heroes. We have had patriots to defend our homes, our liberties, but no aspirants to crowns or thrones; nor have the American people ever suffered themselves to be led on by wicked ambition to depopulate the land, to spread desolation far and wide, that a human being might be placed on a seat of supremacy.

We have no interest in the scenes of antiquity, only as lessons of avoidance of nearly all their examples. The expansive future is our arena, and for our history. We are entering on its untrodden space, with the truths of God in our minds, beneficent objects in our hearts, and with a clear conscience unsullied by the past. We are the nation of human progress, and who will, what can, set limits to our onward march? Providence is with us, and no earthly power can. We point to the everlasting truth on the first page of our national declaration, and we proclaim to the millions of other lands, that "the gates of hell"—the powers of aristocracy and monarchy—"shall not prevail against it."

29. The passage is titled and refers to a concept known as which of the following?

    (1) Communist Manifesto
    (2) Manifest Destiny
    (3) Destined Expansion
    (4) Patriotic Manifestation
    (5) Communism Expanded

30. Which of the following statements best sums up the main idea of this passage?

    (1) America is destined to be patriotic.
    (2) America is so great that it must be America's destiny to expand and progress.
    (3) God will stop America's expansion.
    (4) America will one day have a king or queen.
    (5) America will expand into space.

31. During which of the following centuries was this document most likely written?

    (1) 1600s
    (2) 1700s
    (3) 1800s
    (4) 1900s
    (5) 2000s

Directions: Items 32 and 33 are based on the following passage.

The government of a country plays an active role in foreign trade, or the commerce that is conducted with other countries. It is the goal of the government to make sure each year that the imports do not exceed the exports. The government takes a number of steps each year to balance the amount of imports and exports.

32. Which of the following is the term that sums up the goal of the government mentioned in the passage?

    (1) Deficit spending
    (2) Importation exportation equation
    (3) Imbalance of trade
    (4) Favorable balance of trade
    (5) Foreign trade domestication

33. Which of the following is a tool that could be used by the government to achieve its goal?

    (1) Interest rate increase
    (2) Tax cut
    (3) Tax rate increase
    (4) Printing more money
    (5) Tariff

Directions: Items 34 and 35 are based on the following passage.

The forerunners in this great undertaking often cited the Christianization of lost souls as their greatest motivation. Although many involved truly were motivated by religion, others had their sights set on the untold wealth and treasure of foreign lands. Still others used the promise of fame, power, and glory as their motivations for leaving their friends and families to search the unknown.

34. The best title for the passage is which of the following?

    (1) "Motivations of the Explorers"
    (2) "Reasons to Sponsor Missionaries"
    (3) "Wealthy, Famous Missionaries"
    (4) "Reasons to Leave"
    (5) "Searching for Treasure"

35. The people to whom this passage refers are most likely which of the following?

    (1) Twentieth-century astronauts
    (2) Nineteenth-century pioneers
    (3) Eighteenth-century politicians
    (4) Sixteenth-century explorers
    (5) Thirteenth-century crusaders

Directions: Items 36 and 37 are based on the following passage.

Washington D.C. is home to a number of groups whose sole purpose is to visit politicians and express the ideas and opinions of the companies and organizations who hire them. Every day, people from these groups try to persuade the politicians to set policy and create laws according to the needs and wishes of their clients. Occasionally, these groups are not hired by others but are simply acting based on their own desires, needs, or opinions.

36. The groups of people in the passage are known as which of the following?

    (1) Boosters

    (2) Lawyers

    (3) Lobbyists

    (4) Antagonists

    (5) Voters

37. The politicians referred to in the passage are most likely which of the following?

    (1) Senators or Representatives

    (2) Judges

    (3) Members of an executive agency

    (4) The president and vice president

    (5) The police commissioner and mayor

Directions: Items 38 to 40 are based on the following passage.

In 1965, President Johnson, known as LBJ, retaliated against the forces who attacked an American air base. He ordered bombing raids, and he sent in ground troops. By the end of the year, more than 150,000 U.S. troops were engaged in jungle warfare on the other side of the world. By 1968, a half million troops were bogged down in a fight against communism that was wildly unpopular on the homefront. Massive demonstrations by students and other concerned citizens were a common sight in the streets of America. At some rallies, protesters shouted, "Hey, Hey, LBJ! How

many kids did you kill today?" Not until 1973, under the administration of Richard Nixon, did American troops finally come home.

38. The passage refers to the armed conflict in which of the following countries?

    (1) Japan

    (2) Korea

    (3) Vietnam

    (4) Cuba

    (5) Grenada

39. President Johnson deployed troops through which of his powers?

    (1) Chief of State

    (2) Chief Executive Officer

    (3) Major General

    (4) Commander in Chief

    (5) Chief Diplomat

40. President Johnson did not declare war in this conflict for which of the following reasons?

    (1) Only the Congress can declare war.

    (2) The president can only declare war on large countries.

    (3) Third-world countries are exempt from declared war status.

    (4) American troops were secretly deployed, so there was no reason for a declaration.

    (5) President Johnson actually did declare war, but he was vetoed.

Directions: Items 41 and 42 are based on the following passage.

According to Article IV Section I, each state is required to honor the public records and documents of other states. For example, a California driver's license is valid in every other state. Conversely, a marriage license from any other state is valid in California. In addition, court decisions from one state must be respected by the other states. This article ensures cooperation between the states.

41. This provision is found in which of the following documents?

    (1) Declaration of Independence

    (2) Articles of Confederation

    (3) U.S. Constitution

    (4) Bill of Rights

    (5) Emancipation Proclamation

42. Article IV Section I is also known as which of the following?

    (1) Cooperation Clause

    (2) Full Faith and Credit Clause

    (3) Bill of Rights

    (4) Prohibition

    (5) Emancipation Proclamation

Directions: Items 43 to 45 are based on the following passage.

At the end of the war, the Big Four gathered in France to begin work on a peace treaty. Germany was present at the peace talks, but she had no say in her fate. The treaty was completed in 1919. As a result, the participants in the peace talks blamed Germany for the war. Also, the participants made Germany pay an almost unimaginable amount for reparations for the destruction in the war. Finally, the Germany armed forces were strictly limited in size. Although the Big Four felt better for punishing Germany, Germany was left feeling as if the world had ganged up on her. The United States, one of the Big Four, proposed a plan for a League of Nations, a kind of international peacekeeping coalition. Several other countries joined the League, but the United States did not. Ultimately the League of Nations failed. Many historians argue that the weak peace treaty, the harsh treatment of Germany, and the failure of the League of Nations contributed to the outbreak of the next great war a little over twenty years later.

43. The war mentioned in the passage that ended with the treaty in 1919 was which of the following?

    (1) Spanish American War

    (2) World War I

    (3) World War II

    (4) Russian Revolution

    (5) Korean War

44. The participation of the United States in the peace talks can be considered which of the following?

    (1) Trade negotiations

    (2) Espionage

    (3) International diplomacy

    (4) Domestic policy

    (5) Fiscal policy

45. The U.S. Congress refused to allow the United States to join the League of Nations because member nations were required to go to war if any other member nation were attacked. Congress objected to this policy for which of the following reasons?

    (1) That policy took the power to declare war out of the hands of Congress.

    (2) Congress did not like the other member nations.

    (3) There were no nations left to fight in a war.

    (4) Germany promised not to attack any member nations.

    (5) Congress was in a heated struggle for power with the president.

Directions: Items 46 and 47 are based on the following passage.

The Supreme Court is the highest court in the land. This means that there is no court in the country that has authority or jurisdiction over the Supreme Court. If a case is appealed at a lower court, it goes to a higher court. The last chance a case has on appeal is the U.S. Supreme Court. In addition, once the Supreme Court has made a decision and has issued an opinion, all lower courts, at both the state and federal levels, must abide by the Court's decision.

46. The branch of government described in the passage is which of the following?

    (1) Appellate branch

    (2) Judicial branch

    (3) Executive branch

    (4) Legislative branch

    (5) Administrative branch

47. The fact that there are courts at the state and federal level is an example of which of the following?

    (1) Separation of powers

    (2) Checks and balances

    (3) Appellate procedure

    (4) Federalism

    (5) Nationalism

Directions: Items 48 to 50 are based on the following map.

48. Which of the following states is closest to the equator?

    (1) New Mexico

    (2) North Carolina

    (3) Iowa

    (4) Maine

    (5) Washington

49. Which of the following states is farthest from the Prime Meridian?

    (1) Florida

    (2) Maine

    (3) Texas

    (4) North Dakota

    (5) California

50. Which of the following states lies at approximately 40°N105°W?

    (1) Colorado

    (2) Nevada

    (3) Illinois

    (4) Idaho

    (5) New Mexico

Answer Explanations

26. **The correct answer is (4).** The twelve countries make up the European Union.

27. **The correct answer is (3).** The use of interest rates and monetary control is called monetary policy.

28. **The correct answer is (5).** A mixed economy, or an economy with elements of more than economic system, is best suited for using a currency such as the Euro.

29. **The correct answer is (2).** John O'Sullivan wrote the document called "Manifest Destiny."

30. **The correct answer is (2).** The idea behind Manifest Destiny was that the great nation of the United States could and should expand uninhibited all the way to the Pacific Ocean.

31. **The correct answer is (3).** The idea of Manifest Destiny was popular during the mid-1800s when the United States was aggressively adding territory.

32. **The correct answer is (4).** A favorable balance of trade occurs when the exports equal or exceed the imports of a country.

33. **The correct answer is (5).** A tariff is a tax placed on an import to make its price higher. This makes domestic products more attractive to consumers.

34. **The correct answer is (1).** The passage describes the motives of the European explorers who explored the far corners of the globe during the sixteenth century.

35. **The correct answer is (4).** The people in the passage are most likely the sixteenth-century explorers sent by European monarchs to find new land and treasure.

36. **The correct answer is (3).** Lobbyists are political activists who try to persuade politicians and lawmakers to set policy and make laws according to certain ideas or opinions. Often lobbyists are employed by companies, but some lobbyists work for individuals or organizations.

37. **The correct answer is (1).** The politicians in the passage are most likely Senators or Representatives because these are the lawmakers of the nation and the people that lobbyists must persuade.

38. **The correct answer is (3).** The U.S. became involved in the Vietnam conflict when President Johnson deployed troops there. They did not come until 1973.

39. **The correct answer is (4).** As Commander in Chief, the president can deploy troops.

40. **The correct answer is (1).** Although the president can deploy troops, only Congress can actually declare war on another country.

41. **The correct answer is (3).** The U.S. Constitution contains Article IV Section I.

42. **The correct answer is (2).** Article IV Section I of the U.S. Constitution is also known as the Full Faith and Credit Clause because the article instructs states to issue full faith and credit to the public records, documents, and decisions of all other states.

43. **The correct answer is (2).** The Treaty of Versailles ended World War I.

44. **The correct answer is (3).** International diplomacy is any relations that a country has with other nations concerning trade, peace, or another issue.

45. **The correct answer is (1).** Congress refused to allow the power to declare war pass from its control. By joining the League of Nations, the U.S. would have been locked into a declaration of war if a member nation were attacked.

46. **The correct answer is (2).** The judicial branch of the government includes the courts at every level.

47. **The correct answer is (4).** Federalism is the division of government authority and responsibility into multiple levels such as the local, state, and federal levels.

48. **The correct answer is (1).** New Mexico is the state farthest to the south, so it is closest to the equator.

49. **The correct answer is (5).** California is the farthest west and is therefore the farthest from the Prime Meridian.

50. **The correct answer is (1).** The latitude line 40°N intersects the longitude line 105°W to form a coordinate that lies in the state of Colorado.

Day 23

Science Practice Test (Part I)

For the purposes of this book, the Science Test will be divided into two parts so that you will have time today and tomorrow to answer questions and review the answers in the amount of time you have allotted for GED preparation. For this practice test, give yourself 40 minutes to complete all the questions for Day 23. The GED Science Test will contain 50 questions.

Science Directions

The following are test directions reprinted by permission of the GED Testing Service.

The Science Test consists of multiple-choice questions intended to measure your knowledge of the general concepts in science. The questions are based on short readings that often include a graph, chart, or figure. Study the information given and then answer the question(s) following it. Refer to the information as often as necessary in answering the questions.

You should spend no more than 85 minutes answering the questions in this booklet. Work carefully, but do not spend too much time on any one question. Be sure you answer every question. You will not be penalized for incorrect answers.

Do not mark in this test booklet. Record your answers to the questions on the separate answer sheet provided. Be sure all requested information is properly recorded on the answer sheet.

To record your answers, mark the numbered space on the answer sheet beside the number that corresponds to the question in the test booklet.

FOR EXAMPLE:

Which of the following is the smallest unit in a living thing?

(1) Tissue

(2) Organ

(3) Cell

(4) Muscle

(5) Capillary

The correct answer is cell; therefore, answer space (3) would be marked on the answer sheet.

Do not rest the point of your pencil on the answer sheet while you are considering your answer. Make no stray or unnecessary marks. If you change an answer, erase your first mark completely. Mark only one answer space for each question; multiple answers will be scored as incorrect. Do not fold or crease your answer sheet. Return all test materials to the test administrator.

Directions: Items 1 and 2 are based on the following passage.

Erosion is the process by which rock and soil is moved on the surface of the earth, generally by a natural process. There are five basic ways that erosion can take place. Weathering takes place when the climate of an area affects the land. Hot or cold weather can expand or contract rocks and minerals, causing erosion. Rainy weather can have the effect of leeching the soil of minerals, causing erosion. Wind erosion, especially in arid climates, causes particles of soil and sand to be moved. Sand dunes are caused by the wind blowing. Glacial erosion occurs over a long period of time and removes rock as the glacier melts. Coastal erosion occurs because of the action of the waves of the oceans and is particularly severe during storms. Water erosion occurs when the ground is saturated with moisture. Excess water runs off carrying with it loose soil.

1. One can infer from the passage that erosion in the Sahara Desert is most likely the result of
   (1) weathering.
   (2) coastal erosion.
   (3) wind erosion.
   (4) water erosion.
   (5) glacial erosion.

2. Hurricanes in Florida can, over a period of time, change the shape of its beaches. This is the result of
   (1) coastal erosion.
   (2) wind erosion.
   (3) glacial erosion.
   (4) weathering.
   (5) water erosion.

Directions: Item 3 is based on the following passage.

All Earth's energy is produced through photosynthesis. Photosynthesis is the process by which green plants, algae, and some bacteria take light from the sun and convert it to chemical energy. Only organisms that contain chlorophyll can undergo photosynthesis. Chlorophyll is the pigment that makes plants green. The process of photosynthesis usually occurs in the leaves of plants.

3. From reading the selection, it can be assumed that
   (1) if a plant is not green, it cannot produce energy.
   (2) all living things undergo photosynthesis.
   (3) if a plant does not have leaves, it cannot produce energy.
   (4) on cloudy days, photosynthesis cannot occur.
   (5) photosynthesis does not occur in the winter.

Directions: Items 4 and 5 are based on the following passage.

The smallest unit of an element is an atom. Each atom is made up of a positively charged nucleus that is surrounded by a network of electrons. Atoms combine to form molecules, and every chemical substance is made up of molecules. The distinct way atoms combine in the molecules determines the element. A molecule of water, for example, is made up of two atoms of hydrogen and one atom of oxygen. The symbol for water is H_2O.

In the Periodic Table, all known elements are arranged according to their chemical properties. Elements with similar properties appear together in the table. Besides the symbol for the element, each element has an atomic number associated with it. The weight of the element is indicated by this number. The higher the number, the heavier the element. For example, iron is symbolized by Fe and has the atomic number 26. Mercury is symbolized by Hg and has been assigned the number 80, which means that it is heavier than iron.

4. An element is determined by
   (1) the arrangement of the element in the Periodic Table.
   (2) the combination of atoms in the element.
   (3) the atomic weight of an element.
   (4) how much water is in the element.
   (5) the symbol of the element.

5. The atomic number of an element indicates
   (1) the number of molecules in the element.
   (2) where the element is placed on the Periodic Table.
   (3) the weight of the element.
   (4) the number of atoms combined with molecules in the element.
   (5) the chemical properties of the element.

Directions: Items 6 to 8 are based on the following passage.

The three basic principles of mechanics were formulated by Isaac Newton and are known as Newton's Laws. The first law states that an object will remain in motion or in a state of rest unless something influences it and changes its course. This property is referred to as inertia. If you were sitting in an airplane, the force of the airplane taking off would push you against your seat, overcoming your inertia. The second law states that the change of motion is proportional to the force of change. The greater the applied force, the greater the acceleration. If the same force were applied to two objects, a car and a truck, for example, the truck would show a smaller acceleration. The third law states that for every action (or applied force), there is an equal and opposite reaction. The forward thrust of a rocket, for example, takes place from the force of the expanding gases in the rocket's combustion chamber acting equally in all directions. The thrust is produced by the reaction to the force of expansion on the closed front end of the combustion chamber.

6. An example of Newton's first law would be
   (1) a mother pushing a baby carriage.
   (2) two shopping carts colliding in a grocery store.
   (3) a child falling off a bike.
   (4) allowing air to escape from a balloon.
   (5) the whiplash you would experience in a car by suddenly applying the brake.

7. An example of Newton's second law would be
   (1) a child falling off a bike.
   (2) a mother pushing a baby carriage.
   (3) two shopping carts colliding in a grocery store.
   (4) the whiplash you would experience in a car by suddenly applying the brake.
   (5) allowing air to escape from a balloon.

8. An example of Newton's third law would be
   (1) allowing air to escape from a balloon.
   (2) two shopping carts colliding in a grocery store.
   (3) the whiplash you would experience in a car by suddenly applying the brake.
   (4) a child falling off a bike.
   (5) a mother pushing a baby carriage.

Directions: Items 9 and 10 refer to the following passage.

Metabolism is defined as the total of all the chemical activities of the body's cells. The resting metabolism is the rate at which the body uses up energy while it is at rest. The resting metabolism of different people varies according to their age, sex, body size, and shape. There are people who seem to eat a great deal and never gain weight, while there are others who eat very little and seem to gain weight easily. The basal metabolic rate (BMR) is the measure of the rate of metabolism at rest. Those who tend to have a higher BMR also seem to be people who gain little weight. The BMR is also closely related to the amount of lean tissue a person has. In general, men tend to have more lean tissue than women do. The BMR rises with exercise and decreases with age as the body loses lean tissue. The resting metabolism accounts for as much as half of the energy people use.

9. A person who wants to lose weight

   (1) cannot lose weight without changing the amount of lean tissue in his or her body.

   (2) should eat less.

   (3) should increase the activity of the body's cells.

   (4) can rest more.

   (5) should exercise more to raise the BMR.

10. BMR is defined as

    (1) the rate at which people gain weight.

    (2) the amount of lean tissue a person has.

    (3) the total of all the chemical activities of the body's cells.

    (4) the measure of the rate of metabolism at rest.

    (5) the energy used while exercising.

Directions: Items 11 to14 refer to the following passage.

The human brain is made up of billions of cells called neurons. At birth, the structure of the brain is almost complete, but it continues to grow until about age 20. The major part of the brain is the cerebrum, and it is divided into two hemispheres that are mainly responsible for movement and sensation of one side of the body. The left hemisphere controls the right side of the body, and the right hemisphere controls the left side. Speech is usually controlled by the left hemisphere.

Inside each of the hemispheres is the cortex. Beneath the cortex are the four lobes of each hemisphere. Each lobe is responsible for a different function. The occipital lobes receive and analyze visual information. The temporal lobes deal with sound. The frontal lobes regulate voluntary movement and assist in language. The prefrontal lobes located in the frontal lobes are thought to be involved with intelligence and personality. The parietal lobes are associated with our sense of touch and balance.

11. The brain is

    (1) made up of neurons.

    (2) divided into two hemispheres.

    (3) one large mass.

    (4) another name for the cerebrum.

    (5) another name for the cortex.

12. The size of the brain of a 30-year-old woman is

    (1) the same size it was when she was 12 years old.

    (2) the same size it was when she was 25 years old.

    (3) smaller than it was when she was 25 years old.

    (4) smaller than it will become when she is older.

    (5) different from the size it will be when she is 50 years old.

13. If the frontal lobe were diseased, it would affect a person's

    (1) eyesight.

    (2) personality.

    (3) intelligence.

    (4) language.

    (5) sense of touch.

14. If a right-handed person were to suffer a stroke affecting the left side of his brain, which functions would be involved?

    (1) His speech

    (2) His whole body

    (3) His right hand and his speech

    (4) His right hand

    (5) His left hand

Directions: Items 15 to 17 refer to the following passage.

A comet is made up of small, icy particles and gases. There are three main classes of comets. Short period comets are comets whose cycles only amount to a few years and are faint. Long period comets take decades to travel around the sun and are much easier to see because they are fairly bright. Haley's Comet, which is seen every 76 years, is classified as a long period comet. Finally, there are very long period comets whose cycles are so long, they have yet to be accurately measured. Comets are made up of three parts: a nucleus that contains most of the mass; a coma, or head of the comet; and the tail that is made up of dust and gas. The coma and tail appear when the comet approaches the Sun and solar radiation vaporizes some of the nucleus. Very small comets often do not have tails.

A meteor (or shooting star) is a rapidly moving point of light caused by objects moving at high speeds across the sky. Often a tail is visible on a meteor. A meteor is actually a very small particle that moves around the sun. Because of its extremely high speed, the meteor creates friction with the air molecules, which causes it to destroy itself before it reaches the earth. The visible streak in the sky is caused by its effect on the atmosphere. A sporadic meteor may appear from any direction at any time. Shower meteors are associated with comets.

15. Comets

(1) are very small.

(2) are always precisely measured by their cycles.

(3) are points of light moving across the sky.

(4) often fall to the earth.

(5) cannot always be measured by their cycles.

16. A meteor

(1) never has a tail.

(2) always has a tail.

(3) has a distinct and recognizable path.

(4) does not cause any damage when it falls to Earth.

(5) causes great damage when it falls to Earth.

17. A comet can be distinguished from a meteor by

(1) its speed.

(2) its tail.

(3) its light.

(4) its cycles.

(5) its size.

Directions: Items 18 and 19 refer to the following passage.

Humans have 23 pairs of chromosomes. Twenty-two of the pairs are the same in males and females. The remaining pair is made up of the sex chromosomes. These determine the sex of a baby. Females have two X chromosomes; males have one X chromosome and one Y chromosome. One of the X chromosomes is always inherited from the mother, and either one X or one Y chromosome is inherited from the father.

18. The sex of a baby is determined by

(1) X chromosomes.

(2) Y chromosomes.

(3) the combination of X and Y chromosomes.

(4) the mother's chromosomes.

(5) the number of pairs of chromosomes.

19. A male baby has

(1) three X chromosomes.

(2) two X chromosomes.

(3) two Y chromosomes.

(4) 22 pairs of chromosomes.

(5) one X and one Y chromosome.

Directions: Items 20 and 21 refer to the following passage.

Neurons are the nerve cells that transmit information throughout the body. Each microscopic neuron has its own job, and together, they allow our bodies to be aware of everything we see, hear, taste, and feel. This is accomplished by the neuron sending and receiving electrical signals through a process of chemical exchange or a mechanical stimulus. These signals or messages are channeled through the brain. Sensory neurons are responsible for transmitting messages to the brain and the spinal cord. Motor neurons carry commands from the brain and spinal cord to the muscles and glands. Interneurons send signals back and forth between the brain and spinal cord to other parts of the body. The process of sending messages takes only a fraction of a second.

20. A pin prick to the finger would be classified as

    (1) an electrical signal.

    (2) a mechanical stimulus.

    (3) a sensory neuron.

    (4) a neuron sending a message.

    (5) an chemical exchange.

21. The ability to smell a flower is a result of

    (1) interneurons sending signals to the spinal cord.

    (2) chemical reaction stimulating sensory neurons.

    (3) electrical stimuli.

    (4) motor neurons stimulated by a mechanical stimulus.

    (5) motor neurons stimulated by the flower.

Directions: Items 22 to 24 refer to the following passage.

There are three forms in which matter occurs: solid, liquid, and gas. Solid matter generally does not change its shape, liquid matter generally does not resist a force to change its shape, and gas that is not contained will diffuse into the air indefinitely and become weaker as it is diffused. Temperature of a substance, however, can change its form.

22. Ice placed into a pot and boiled is an example of

    (1) a solid changing to a gas.

    (2) a solid changing to a liquid.

    (3) a liquid changing to a solid.

    (4) a liquid changing to a gas.

    (5) a liquid state of matter.

23. When a plastic bag is recycled to make a soda container, it goes from

    (1) a liquid to solid state.

    (2) a solid to liquid to gas state.

    (3) a solid to gas to liquid state.

    (4) a solid to liquid to solid state.

    (5) a gas to solid state.

Directions: Items 24 and 25 refer to the following passage.

Sound is a form of energy that is produced when an object vibrates and a medium, such as air, vibrates in response. As an object vibrates, it sets the air molecules around it vibrating. A region of higher pressure, or compression, of molecules forms around the vibration. An area of lower pressure, or rarefaction, occurs where the molecules move apart. A sound wave is formed as the compressions and rarefactions move through the air. The farther apart the rarefactions and compressions, the lower the sound. Although sound waves generally travel in straight lines, a sound wave can be reflected when it strikes a surface or diffracted as it passes through an opening. Sound is measured in decibels. The frequency of the vibration of a sound wave is measured in hertz. The range of frequencies for hearing of human beings usually lies between 20 and 20,000 hertz. Sound above this range for man is called ultrasound.

24. If you are sitting in a room with the doors and windows closed, you can still hear sound because of

    (1) reflection.

    (2) ultrasound.

    (3) compression.

    (4) diffraction.

    (5) the frequency of vibration of the sound.

25. A sound wave is the result of

    (1) reflection.

    (2) rarefactions.

    (3) compression.

    (4) diffraction.

    (5) compression and rarefactions.

Answer Explanations

1. **The correct answer is (3).** The wind plays a greater role in eroding the desert because the wind blows the sand and creates the dunes.

2. **The correct answer is (1).** Because hurricanes are storms of great magnitude, they are responsible for the coastal erosion that can change the shape of Florida's beaches.

3. **The correct answer is (1).** Photosynthesis can only occur in green plants.

4. **The correct answer is (2).** Atoms make up molecules, so it is the unique combination of atoms that determines an element.

5. **The correct answer is (3).** In the Periodic Table, each element is assigned a number to indicate the weight of the element.

6. **The correct answer is (5).** Applying the brakes suddenly to a car would cause the passengers to violently move forward; and as the car stops, they would violently move backward, causing whiplash.

7. **The correct answer is (2).** The force the mother uses to push the carriage is proportional to how fast the carriage moves.

8. **The correct answer is (1).** The balloon would be propelled into the air by the force of the air escaping. The action of the balloon being propelled into the air is a result of the opposite reaction.

9. **The correct answer is (5).** BMR rises with exercise, and because metabolism is defined as the rate at which the body burns energy, raising the level of exercise would cause an increase in metabolism, causing a person to lose weight more efficiently.

10. **The correct answer is (4).** BMR (basic metabolic rate) is tested and interpreted as the rate of a person's metabolism while at rest.

11. **The correct answer is (1).** The cells that make up the brain are called neurons.

12. **The correct answer is (2).** The human brain continues to grow from birth until about age 20. Because of this, there would be no change in size or development of the brain between the ages of 25 and 30.

13. **The correct answer is (4).** The frontal lobes regulate voluntary movement and assist in language development, so a disease affecting the frontal lobes could affect a person's language functions.

14. **The correct answer is (3).** If a right-handed person suffered a stroke that affected the left side of his brain, his right hand and his speech would also be affected because the left hemisphere controls both the right side of the body as well as speech.

15. **The correct answer is (5).** Because some comets have very long periods or cycles, sometimes spanning decades, their cycles have not all been accurately identified yet.

16. **The correct answer is (4).** A meteor is a very small particle point of light that destroys itself through the process of friction before it falls to the earth, so it does not cause damage.

17. **The correct answer is (4).** A meteor can appear from any direction at any time and burns itself out. A comet, however, has a distinct cycle of movement around the sun.

18. **The correct answer is (3).** The specific combination of chromosomes determines the sex of a baby.

19. **The correct answer is (5).** There is one pair of sex chromosomes. Females have two X chromosomes, and males have one X and one Y chromosome.

20. **The correct answer is (2).** A pin prick is a mechanical stimulus that affects the neurons in the finger. These neurons send a message to the brain telling it to feel the pain inflicted by the pin prick.

21. **The correct answer is (2).** Scent riggers a chemical reaction that stimulates the sensory neurons in the nose.

22. **The correct answer is (1).** The ice begins as a solid, and as it heats, it changes to a liquid. Finally, as it begins to boil, it changes to a steam, which is a gas released into the air.

23. **The correct answer is (4).** The plastic bag begins as a solid, and as it is heated, it melts and changes

to a liquid. Finally, when it is formed into a soda container, it becomes a solid again.

24. **The correct answer is (1).** Sound waves generally travel in a straight line, but when waves encounter a surface such as a wall, they are reflected. The sound will not be as loud as it was originally, but in many cases, it can still be heard.

25. **The correct answer is (5).** A sound wave requires both compression of molecules or high pressure and an area of lower pressure or rarefaction where molecules move farther apart.

Day 24

Science Practice Test (Part II)

For the purposes of this book, the Science Test will be divided into two parts so that you will have time today and tomorrow to answer questions and review the answers in the amount of time you have allotted for GED preparation. For this practice test, give yourself 40 minutes to complete all the questions for Day 24. The GED Science Test will contain 50 questions.

Science Directions

The following are test directions reprinted by permission of the GED Testing Service.

The Science Test consists of multiple-choice questions intended to measure your knowledge of the general concepts in science. The questions are based on short readings that often include a graph, chart, or figure. Study the information given and then answer the question(s) following it. Refer to the information as often as necessary in answering the questions.

You should spend no more than 85 minutes answering the questions in this booklet. Work carefully, but do not spend too much time on any one question. Be sure you answer every question. You will not be penalized for incorrect answers.

Do not mark in this test booklet. Record your answers to the questions on the separate answer sheet provided. Be sure all requested information is properly recorded on the answer sheet.

To record your answers, mark the numbered space on the answer sheet beside the number that corresponds to the question in the test booklet.

FOR EXAMPLE:

Which of the following is the smallest unit in a living thing?

(1) Tissue

(2) Organ

(3) Cell

(4) Muscle

(5) Capillary

The correct answer is cell; therefore, answer space (3) would be marked on the answer sheet.

Do not rest the point of your pencil on the answer sheet while you are considering your answer. Make no stray or unnecessary marks. If you change an answer, erase your first mark completely. Mark only one answer space for each question; multiple answers will be scored as incorrect. Do not fold or crease your answer sheet. Return all test materials to the test administrator.

Directions: Item 1 is based on the following passage.

The human eye contains cells in the retina, called rods, that register black and white. Other retinal cells, called the cones, are affected by color. Electrical signals from the rods and the cones are sent to the front of the retina. Signals are eventually sent to the brain where they are interpreted and perceived as visual images. Many mammals see the world only in black and white images.

1.   It can be assumed that
 (1) electrical signals in many mammals are blocked so they can only see in black and white.
 (2) many mammals do not have cones in their retinas.
 (3) many mammals have more rods than cones in their retinas.
 (4) humans are not mammals.
 (5) many mammals do not have retinas.

Directions: Items 2 and 3 are based on the following passage.

A food web is made up of linking food chains. The two basic types of food webs are the grazing web and the detrital web. In the grazing web, the chain begins with plants that are passed to herbivores (plant eaters) and then carnivores (flesh eaters) or omnivores (those that eat both plants and animals). For example, cows, which are herbivores, eat grass, and humans are omnivores who, in turn, might eat beef products.

The detrital web begins with plant and animal matter that become decomposers (bacteria and fungi). The decomposers then pass to detritivores (organisms that feed on decomposed matter) and then to carnivores. In this web, the decomposed matter is fed upon by earthworms for example, and some species of birds will eat the worms. The predators that feed upon birds are carnivores.

The two webs can overlap because animals could eat the plants that grow in the decomposed matter, and some animals are both plant and flesh eaters.

2.   A carnivore eats
 (1) only animals.
 (2) only plants.
 (3) both plants and animals.
 (4) plants and decomposers.
 (5) plants, animals, and decomposers.

3.   The main idea of this selection is
 (1) vegetarians don't eat meat.
 (2) decomposed matter is eaten by omnivores.
 (3) animals only fit into the grazing web.
 (4) food webs are separate and distinct.
 (5) the detrital web overlaps into the grazing web.

4.   Temperature levels fall from ground level to the top of the troposphere, but they rise in the stratosphere. Which of the following would best account for the rise in temperature?
 (1) Global warming
 (2) Thinner air at higher altitudes
 (3) More gasses in the air at higher altitudes
 (4) The troposphere blocking the rays of the sun
 (5) The ozone layer absorbing heat

5.   A fluid can exert a buoyant force as well as an internal force because of the weight of the fluid above it. The suit of a deep-sea diver must contain a jacket of compressed air whose pressure counteracts the external water pressure. The reason for the jacket of compressed air is
 (1) to allow the diver to go to a greater depth.
 (2) to give the diver an extra source of air.
 (3) to allow the diver to breath without his muscles having to expand his chest against the pressure.
 (4) to make the diver more buoyant in the water.
 (5) to keep the diver from drowning in case there is a leak in his suit.

Directions: Items 6 and 7 refer to the following passage.

Scientific Method is the procedure scientists use to design and conduct an experiment. There are seven steps to this procedure: state the problem or ask a question; research the subject; form a hypothesis (based on research, try to predict a solution or answer); plan and conduct an experiment using an experimental group (the test group known as the variable) and a control group (not exposed to the variable); observe, measure, and record the findings; draw conclusions from the findings; and repeat the experiment for validity.

6. A scientist wanted to see the effects of sunlight on plants. He developed two groups of plants. Group 1 was exposed to the sun for several hours each day, and Group 2 was only exposed to the sun for 2 hours each day. In this experiment, Group 2 was the

    (1) control group.
    (2) variable.
    (3) hypothesis.
    (4) experiment.
    (5) observation.

7. The scientist repeated his experiment on the two groups of plants. The purpose of repeating the experiment was

    (1) to make the experiment fit the hypothesis.
    (2) to make sure he didn't make any mistakes.
    (3) to ensure that he could answer any question.
    (4) to ensure that the test and his conclusions were accurate.
    (5) to ensure that all the plants were growing properly.

Directions: Items 8 to 10 refer to the following selection.

Weather is comprised of air temperature, barometric pressure, wind velocity, humidity clouds, and precipitation. Weather depends on the movements of large air masses that vary in temperature and humidity according to the land or water surface beneath them, and they shift slowly over the surface of the earth. Static masses account for steady weather conditions. Other masses that are affected by the earth's rotation move rapidly and interact with other air masses. These masses account for changeable weather. Most of North America's weather depends on a west to east movement of air masses and the fronts associated with them.

The climate of an area is the long-term weather associated with the area. Besides being influenced by the air masses, it is influenced by the relative distribution of land and water, high and low ground, and the presence of major features such as forests and lakes. Tropical climates are hot, temperate climates are variable, and polar climates are cold.

8. The climate of the South Pole would most likely be

    (1) polar.
    (2) cloudy.
    (3) temperate.
    (4) variable.
    (5) predicted in a west to east movement.

9. Weather depends on

    (1) climate.
    (2) distribution of land and water.
    (3) movement of air masses.
    (4) a west to east movement.
    (5) temperature and precipitation.

10. North America would most likely have

    (1) static air masses.
    (2) long-term weather.
    (3) a variable climate.
    (4) steady weather conditions.
    (5) a temperate climate.

Directions: Items 11 and 12 are based on the following diagram.

11. Which of the following would be the best title for the illustration?

    (1) "The Food Chain"

    (2) "Osmosis"

    (3) "Photosynthesis"

    (4) "Digestion"

    (5) "Vegetative Interaction"

12. Which of the following makes possible the process in the illustration?

    (1) Cell membranes

    (2) Chlorophyll

    (3) Enzymes

    (4) Ozone

    (5) Oxygen

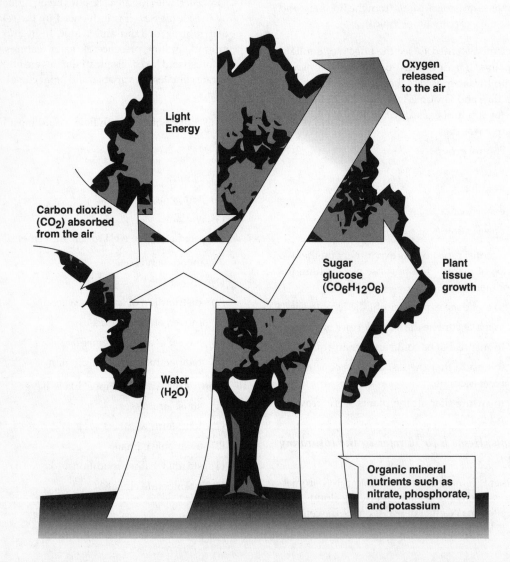

13. Atoms are made up of protons and neutrons that are closely packed in the nucleus of the atom. The third component of an atom is the electron. The electrons are spread out more than the protons and neutrons, and much of an atom is comprised of empty space. The electrons are located outside the central nucleus. When two atoms collide, it is most likely that

    (1) the protons and neutrons will come into contact with each other.

    (2) the protons will come into contact with the nuclei.

    (3) the electrons will come into contact with each other.

    (4) the nuclei will come into contact with each other.

    (5) the electrons and the nuclei will come into contact with each other.

Directions: Items 14 and15 refer to the following passage.

Most solid matter is composed of crystals. The most obvious crystals we are familiar with are sugar and salt. It is often difficult to identify materials as being composed of crystals since a large number of them have been aggregated to produce the substance. Crystals grow by precipitation out of a solution or a cooling melt. The atoms or ions cluster into small "seeds" and continue to build in layers.

Minerals are naturally occurring inorganic substances made up of one or more elements, and most are crystalline. A mineral is identified by the crystal shape as well as the cleavage (the way the mineral breaks), the hardness, the color, and the luster (the way in which the light is reflected).

14. You can infer from the passage that

    (1) sugar is a mineral.

    (2) not all crystals are minerals.

    (3) if you leave a crystal in the rain, it will grow.

    (4) melted crystals form minerals.

    (5) if a substance doesn't have a luster, it is not a mineral.

15. Which of the following is NOT an identifying factor of a mineral?

    (1) The crystal shape

    (2) The hardness

    (3) The cleavage

    (4) The solution out of which it grew

    (5) The luster

Directions: Items 16 and 17 refer to the following passage.

The raw materials that make up all plants are water, carbon dioxide, and sunlight. Plants have no nervous system, and their growth is controlled by the release of hormonal materials. All plants manufacture their own food using oxygen and releasing carbon dioxide. There are two basic groups of plants: seed bearing and non-seed bearing. In the seed bearing group are flowing plants and most trees. An example of non-seed bearing plants are mosses. Among the seed bearing plants are annuals that can have a very rapid life cycle and perennials that can live to a great age.

16. Trees are considered

    (1) flowing plants.

    (2) annuals.

    (3) perennials.

    (4) non-seed bearing.

    (5) seed bearing annuals.

17. Because plants do not have a nervous system, they

    (1) do not grow.

    (2) cannot manufacture food.

    (3) need sunlight to grow.

    (4) are not considered to be living things.

    (5) have their growth controlled by hormonal substances.

18. Like Earth, Mercury, the smallest planet, revolves around the Sun. It takes nearly 88 days to make one revolution around the Sun. Earth takes 365 days to complete one revolution around the Sun. Earth completes one revolution on its own axis in 24 hours, or one day. Mercury, on the other hand, takes 58.5 Earth days to slowly make one turn on its axis. As a result,

    (1) the surface of Mercury is alternately baked by the Sun and frozen by outer space for long periods.

    (2) Mercury has shorter days than Earth.

    (3) Earth passes it in its revolutions around the Sun.

    (4) Mercury travels around the Sun at a slower rate than Earth does.

    (5) as compared to an Earth year, Mercury's year is longer.

Directions: Items 19 and 20 refer to the following selection.

Cholesterol is a substance that is essential for proper function of the cells in humans. It is carried through the body in the bloodstream by lipoproteins. The majority of the cholesterol in the blood is bound to low-density lipoprotein (LDL) and is referred to as LDL cholesterol. This is the major contributor to overall cholesterol levels. The higher this level, the more risk a person has of coronary artery disease. The remaining cholesterol is bound to high-density lipoprotein (HDL). HDL cholesterol actually seem to protect against the risk of coronary artery disease and lowers overall cholesterol. Most of a person's cholesterol is produced by the liver. A great deal of saturated fat in one's diet encourages the liver to produce large amounts of cholesterol.

19. You can infer from this passage that

    (1) all fats are bad for the body.

    (2) coronary artery disease is inescapable.

    (3) all cholesterol in the blood is bad.

    (4) since cholesterol is produced in the liver, no one can control the levels of cholesterol.

    (5) lowering your intake of saturated fats could help you control your cholesterol level.

20. People can help to protect themselves from coronary artery disease by

    (1) only eating saturated fats.

    (2) not eating any fat in their diet.

    (3) taking injections of high-density cholesterol.

    (4) increasing the amount of HDL cholesterol.

    (5) increasing the amount of LDL cholesterol.

21. Three types of processes are used for separating a metal from the waste rock in which it is embedded. Mechanical separation employs gravity to remove waste materials, flotation mixes ground ore with a liquid and the waste that is heavier than the ore is dispensed, and electrostatic separation relies on the attraction of unlike charges and the repulsion of like charges for the separation process. Which process explains how one pans for gold?

    (1) Electrostatic

    (2) Mechanical

    (3) Flotation

    (4) A combination of flotation and electrostatic

    (5) A combination of mechanical and flotation

22. Solar collectors provide energy for buildings by pumping water through panels mounted on the roof. The water picks up heat from the sun, and the pump is controlled by a sensor so it operates when the collector is several degrees hotter than the water in the storage tank. This type of energy would work best in

    (1) the Northeast.

    (2) the Northwest.

    (3) the Southwest.

    (4) the Great Lakes area.

    (5) anywhere in the country.

Directions: Items 23 and 24 refer to the following passage.

Nearsightedness, or myopia, is the condition of the eye that causes distant objects to appear blurry. In this condition, the light that enters the eye is focusing in front of the retina instead of precisely on the retina. This condition can be corrected with the use of concave lenses.

Farsightedness, or hypermetropia, is the condition of the eye that causes close objects to appear blurry while distant objects are more clearly focused. In this condition, light rays are focusing behind the retina. This condition can be corrected with the use of convex lenses. The ability to focus on close objects diminishes with age.

23. People who require reading glasses

    (1) are old.

    (2) have hypermetropia.

    (3) have concave lenses in the glasses.

    (4) have retinas that do not focus.

    (5) cannot see distant objects.

24. Contact lenses would be most appropriate for

    (1) people who are old.

    (2) anyone with blurry vision.

    (3) people who suffer from myopia.

    (4) people who have either hypermetropia or myopia.

    (5) people who suffer from hypermetropia.

Directions: Item 25 refers to the following selection.

There are three types of rocks on the earth's surface: igneous, metamorphic, and sedimentary. Igneous rocks have been formed by the cooling of molten magma where temperatures are extremely high. Metamorphic rocks have been formed by the compression of older rocks. They are formed below the surface of the earth where both the temperature and pressure are high. Sedimentary rocks are formed by weathering or the remains of living organisms. These are formed on the surface of the earth under low pressures.

25. One can infer from this passage that the three types of rocks

    (1) can be found anywhere.

    (2) are all approximately the same age.

    (3) are all located in different places on the earth.

    (4) share common characteristics.

    (5) will all look the same.

Answer Explanations

1. **The correct answer is (2).** The many mammals that can only see in black and white are lacking cones. Cones are the cells that enable the eye to distinguish color.

2. **The correct answer is (1).** A carnivore eats only meat.

3. **The correct answer is (5).** Food chains link to form webs; decomposed matter, which is made up of plant and animal matter, is consumed by herbivores, and they in turn can be consumed by carnivores, which results in an overlapping of food chains.

4. **The correct answer is (5).** The stratosphere is closer to the ozone layer than the troposphere, so the effect of the ozone layer would be to raise the temperatures closer to the top of the layer.

5. **The correct answer is (3).** The compressed air of the diver's jacket protects the diver by forming a bubble of air around him that acts as a cushion against the pressure of the water, allowing him to breathe and expand his chest.

6. **The correct answer is (2).** Group 2 was the variable because it was in the test group.

7. **The correct answer is (4).** The Scientific Method requires that the hypothesis be tested several times in order to prove that it is supported.

8. **The correct answer is (1).** The South Pole would experience a polar climate even though the temperatures may vary.

9. **The correct answer is (3).** Weather depends on the movement of air masses, which are affected by the landforms below them.

10. **The correct answer is (3).** The climate of North America would be considered variable because it is neither polar nor tropical.

11. **The correct answer is (3).** The process in which plants change carbon dioxide and sunlight to sugars and oxygen is called photosynthesis.

12. **The correct answer is (2).** Only green plants contain chlorophyll, the pigment necessary for the photosynthesis process.

13. **The correct answer is (3).** Because the electrons are located outside the central nucleus of an atom and because they are spread out in the surrounding space, they would be more likely to collide than the nuclei that are embedded inside the atom.

14. **The correct answer is (2).** Although minerals are made up of one or more elements, by definition, not all include crystals.

15. **The correct answer is (4).** The identifying factors of a mineral are its crystal shape, its cleavage, its hardness, its color, and its luster.

16. **The correct answer is (3).** Seed bearing plants can be either annuals or perennials. Because trees continue to grow year after year, they are considered perennials.

17. **The correct answer is (5).** Plants produce their own food and so produce their own hormonal substances, which are responsible for their growth.

18. **The correct answer is (1).** The surface of Mercury is alternately baked by the Sun and frozen by outer space for long periods of time because it takes 58.5 Earth days to make one turn on its axis. This means that it would be facing either the Sun or outer space for approximately 29 hours at a time.

19. **The correct answer is (5).** Because a large amount of saturated fat encourages the liver to produce more cholesterol, lowering your intake of saturated fats would inhibit this process in the liver.

20. **The correct answer is (4).** Because HDL cholesterol actually seems to protect against coronary artery disease, increasing this substance would help to ensure that coronary artery disease would not occur.

21. **The correct answer is (2).** Panning for gold is a mechanical process, since gravity is used in a sieve to remove waste materials from gold nuggets.

22. **The correct answer is (3).** Because the water in a solar collector is heated by the sun, the areas of the country with the warmer climates would make solar energy most efficient.

23. **The correct answer is (2).** Hypermetropia is the condition of the eye that causes close objects to

appear blurry, so those with this condition would have difficulty reading the print in a book.

24. **The correct answer is (3).** Because contact lenses have a concave shape, they would be most appropriate for a person who suffers from myopia.

25. **The correct answer is (3).** Because the three types of rocks are all formed differently under different conditions, they cannot all be found in the same locations.

Day 25

Language Arts, Reading Practice Test (Part I)

For the purposes of this book, the Language Arts, Reading Test will be divided into two parts so that you will have time today and tomorrow to answer questions and review the answers in the amount of time you have allotted for GED preparation. For this practice test, give yourself 32 minutes to complete all the questions for Day 25. The GED Language Arts, Reading Test will contain 40 questions.

Language Arts, Reading Directions

The following are test directions reprinted by permission of the GED Testing Service.

The Language Arts, Reading Test consists of excerpts from fiction and nonfiction. Each excerpt is followed by multiple-choice questions about the reading material.

Read each excerpt first and then answer the questions following it. Refer back to the reading material as often as necessary in answering the questions.

Each excerpt is preceded by a "purpose question." The purpose question gives a reason for reading the material. Use these purpose questions to help focus your reading. You are not required to answer these purpose questions. They are given only to help you concentrate on the ideas presented in the reading material.

You will have 65 minutes to answer the 40 questions in this booklet. Work carefully, but do not spend too much time on any one question. Be sure that all requested information is properly recorded on the answer sheet.

Do not mark in this test booklet. Record your answers on the separate answer sheet provided. Be sure that all requested information is properly recorded on the answer sheet.

To record your answers, fill in the numbered circle on the answer sheet that corresponds to the answer you select for each question in the test booklet.

FOR EXAMPLE:

It was Susan's dream machine. The metallic blue paint gleamed, and the sporty wheels were highly polished. Under the hood, the engine was no less carefully cleaned. Inside, flashy lights illuminated the instruments on the dashboard, and the seats were covered by rich leather upholstery.

The subject (it) of this excerpt is most likely

(1) an airplane.

(2) a stereo system.

(3) an automobile.

(4) a boat.

(5) a motorcycle.

The correct answer is an automobile; therefore, answer space (3) would be marked on the answer sheet.

Do not rest the point of your pencil on the answer sheet while you are considering your answer. Make no stray or unnecessary marks. If you change an answer, erase your first mark completely. Mark only one answer space for each question; multiple answers will be scored as incorrect. Do not fold or crease your answer sheet. All test materials must be returned to the test administrator.

Directions: Items 1 to 6 are based on the following poem by William Shakespeare.

What is the author trying to say?

Tired with all these, for restful death I cry,
As, to behold desert a beggar born,
And needy nothing trimm'd in jollity,
And purest faith unhappily forsworn,
And gilded honour shamefully misplac'd,
And maiden virtue rudely strumpeted,
And right perfection wrongfully disgrac'd,
And strength by limping sway disabled,
And art made tongue-tied by authority,
And folly, doctor-like, controlling skill,
And simple truth miscall'd simplicity,
And captive good attending captain ill:
   Tir'd with all these, from these would I be gone,
   Save that, to die, I leave my love alone.

1. Which of the following best describes the mood of this poem?

(1) Cheery

(2) Thankful

(3) Dark

(4) Optimistic

(5) Light

2. Which of the following states a reason for which the author does not desire to die?

(1) Art

(2) Truth

(3) Virtue

(4) Faith

(5) Love

3. The line, "And art made tongue-tied by authority," most likely means what?

(1) The author does not like art.

(2) The author is frustrated because no one will buy his art.

(3) The author believes that expression through art is limited by bureaucracy.

(4) The author was deaf.

(5) The author was mute.

4. Which of the following best describes the main idea of the poem?

(1) The author is complaining about life.

(2) The author is reminiscing about his life.

(3) The author is dreaming of a future life.

(4) The author is wishing for a better life.

(5) The author is describing someone else's life.

5. Which of the following best characterizes the symbolism of the line, "And captive good attending captain ill"?

(1) "Captive good" describes doctors, and "captain ill" describes sick people.

(2) "Captive good" represents the idea that universal good is enslaved, and "captain ill" represents the evil that has enslaved it.

(3) "Captain ill" represents the captain of a ship.

(4) "Captive good" represents the common man.

(5) "Captain ill" describes the government.

6. Which of the following would be the best title for this poem?

    (1) "Wishing For A Better Life"

    (2) "How I Mourn For My Lost Love"

    (3) "Without These Things, Life Would Be Without Meaning"

    (4) "Tired With All These, For Restful Death I Cry"

    (5) "For Art, Truth, and Faith Do I Live"

Directions: Items 7 to 12 are based on the following passage, excerpts of **Don Quixote** *by* **Cervantes.**

What kind of man is the main character?

In a village of La Mancha, the name of which I have no desire to call to mind, there lived not long since one of those gentlemen that keep a lance in the lance-rack, an old buckler, a lean hack, and a greyhound for coursing...

You must know, then, that the above-named gentleman whenever he was at leisure (which was mostly all the year round) gave himself up to reading books of chivalry with such ardor and avidity that he almost entirely neglected the pursuit of his field-sports, and even the management of his property; and to such a pitch did his eagerness and infatuation go that he sold many an acre of tillage-land to buy books of chivalry to read, and brought home as many of them as he could get...

...His fancy grew full of what he used to read about in his books, enchantments, quarrels, battles, challenges, wounds, wooings, loves, agonies, and all sorts of impossible nonsense; and it so possessed his mind that the whole fabric of invention and fancy he read of was true, that to him no history in the world had more reality in it.

In short, his wits being quite gone, he hit upon the strangest notion that ever madman in this world hit upon, and that was that he fancied it was right and requisite, as well for the support of his own honor as for the service of his country, that he should make a knight-errant of himself, roaming the world over in full armor and on horseback in quest of adventures, and putting in practice himself all that he had read of as being the usual practice of knights-errant; righting every kind of wrong, and exposing himself to peril and danger from which, in the issue, he was to reap eternal renown and fame.

7. In the passage, the line "one of those gentlemen that keep a lance in the lance-rack" refers to which of the following?

    (1) A doctor

    (2) A lawyer

    (3) A knight

    (4) A musician

    (5) A king

8. Which of the following is a true statement about the man described in the passage?

    (1) The man liked books, but he could not read.

    (2) The man owned a bookstore.

    (3) The man borrowed books whenever he could.

    (4) The man loved books, and he loved to read about chivalry.

    (5) The man taught others in the village to read.

9. Which of the following can be said about the man's mental state based on the information in the passage?

    (1) The man had gone crazy.

    (2) The man was a genius.

    (3) The man had the intelligence of a child.

    (4) The man was mad at someone.

    (5) The man was mad because he couldn't get books.

10. Based on the context of the passage, which of the following is the best definition for "knight-errant"?

    (1) A knight who reads

    (2) A knight who performs tasks

    (3) A knight who fights dragons

    (4) A knight who is a knight by mistake

    (5) A knight who makes mistakes

11. Based on the passage, which of the following is most likely to be the plot of the story?

    (1) The man becomes a bookseller and sells all the books he's collected.

    (2) The man becomes famous for his book collection.

    (3) The man becomes a knight and has many adventures.

    (4) The man becomes an author and writes about knights.

    (5) The man becomes a farmer and tills his land.

12. Which of the following is the main idea of the passage?

    (1) The main character is so obsessed with reading about knights that fantasy becomes reality for him.

    (2) The main character is a knight who loves to read about other knights.

    (3) Books have such power that they can drive a man mad.

    (4) Knights are one of the most popular topics for books.

    (5) It is important for knights to read so that they are prepared for whatever tasks they face.

Directions: Items 13 to 16 are based on the following document.

Why was this memo sent to employees?

From: J.R. Smith, Manager, Smith and Smith Service Company

To: Smith and Smith Service Company Employees

In light of recent time card punching practices of some Smith and Smith Service Company employees, management has instituted a new time card punching procedure for all employees. This new procedure will take effect on March 1, 2002 for all non-salaried employees. The new procedure is as follows:

1. Each employee should arrive at the Smith and Smith building no more than 15 minutes before and no later than 5 minutes before shift begins. Upon arrival, each employee should avoid loitering. Each employee should report to the floor manager's office as soon as possible after arriving at the Smith and Smith building.

2. Each employee must punch his or her time card no more than 5 minutes before shift begins and no later than 2 minutes after shift begins.

3. Each employee must punch his or her time card no more than 2 minutes before or 5 minutes after shift ends.

4. If an employee is discovered punching another employee's time card, both employees may be subject to suspension.

5. If an employee punches in before the permitted punch-in time or punches out after the permitted punch-out time more than twice in a 30-day period or more than four times in a 90-day period, the employee may be subject to suspension.

6. An employee's failure to punch a time card for a shift may result in a punitive reduction of wages for that shift.

7. Any actions concerning the time clock by an employee that may be considered by management as fraudulent or malicious may be grounds for termination and/or prosecution.

13. Which of the following can best sum up the main idea of the document?

   (1) The management is looking for an employee who has defrauded the company.

   (2) The management has tried many different things in the past to curb fraudulent behavior by its employees.

   (3) The management has a new policy for its employees that is designed to guide its employees toward appropriate actions concerning the time clock.

   (4) The management wants to suspend employees so that it does not have to pay them.

   (5) The management is biased against non-salaried employees.

14. Which of the following best describe the tone of the document?

   (1) Irate and irrational

   (2) Emotionally charged

   (3) Matter of fact

   (4) Accusatory and suspicious

   (5) Malicious

15. Based on the information in the document, which of the following statements is most likely true?

   (1) Smith and Smith Company employees never misuse the time clock.

   (2) The Smith and Smith Company is notorious for abusing its employees.

   (3) The Smith and Smith Company has never had a time clock for employees to punch their time cards.

   (4) Employees of the Smith and Smith Company are notorious for abusing and breaking rules and regulations.

   (5) Some employees of the Smith and Smith Company have exercised poor judgment regarding the time clock and time card procedure, and this poor judgment has caused problems for the Smith and Smith Company.

16. To which of the following employees would this memo most probably not apply?

   (1) The assembly line workers

   (2) The janitorial staff

   (3) The maintenance staff

   (4) The receptionist

   (5) The accountant

Directions: Items 17 to 20 are based on the following passage, excerpts from "An Occurrence at Owl Creek Bridge" by Ambrose Bierce.

What is actually happening in this story?

Doubtless, despite his suffering, he had fallen asleep while walking, for now he sees another scene—perhaps he has merely recovered from a delirium. He stands at the gate of his own home. All is as he left it, and all bright and beautiful in the morning sunshine. He must have traveled the entire night. As he pushes open the gate and passes up the wide white walk, he sees a flutter of female garments; his wife, looking fresh and cool and sweet, steps down from the veranda to meet him. At the bottom of the steps she stands waiting, with a smile of ineffable joy, an attitude of matchless grace and dignity. Ah, how beautiful she is! He springs forwards with extended arms. As he is about to clasp her he feels a stunning blow upon the back of the neck; a blinding white light blazes all about him with a sound like the shock of a cannon—then all is darkness and silence!

Peyton Fahrquhar was dead; his body, with a broken neck, swung gently from side to side beneath the timbers of the Owl Creek Bridge.

17. Which of the following lines from the passage is an example of a simile?

    (1) "a blinding white light"

    (2) "bright and beautiful in the morning sunshine"

    (3) "ineffable joy"

    (4) "like the shock of a cannon"

    (5) "a stunning blow"

18. Which of the following is the best summary of what actually happened to Peyton Fahrquhar?

    (1) He was kidnapped from his home and then executed.

    (2) He imagined seeing his home and wife as he was executed.

    (3) He was delirious after a cannon fired.

    (4) He imagined the scene after being struck by a cannon blow.

    (5) Peyton Fahrquhar is not the person mentioned in the first paragraph.

19. Based on the information in the passage, which of the following most likely occurred before the action in the first paragraph?

    (1) Peyton Fahrquhar was injured somehow.

    (2) Peyton Fahrquhar died.

    (3) Peyton Fahrquhar fell asleep at his home.

    (4) Peyton Fahrquhar forgot how beautiful his wife was.

    (5) Peyton Fahrquhar robbed a bank.

20. Which of the following is true of the passage?

    (1) The passage is written in first person.

    (2) The passage is written in third person.

    (3) The author uses alliteration frequently throughout the passage.

    (4) The author uses onomatopoeia frequently throughout the passage.

    (5) The author uses a battlefield as the setting of the story.

Answer Explanations

1. **The correct answer is (3).** This poem has a very dark and sad mood, especially since the theme revolves around death and dying.

2. **The correct answer is (5).** The author states that the only reason that he does not want to die is for his love. His love, therefore, is the only factor motivating the author not to die.

3. **The correct answer is (3).** The author uses this language to say that the government limits his ability to express himself freely.

4. **The correct answer is (1).** The author is complaining about all the problems with life and with being alive.

5. **The correct answer is (2).** The author uses this symbolic language to say that even the good in life has been tainted because good often is overpowered by and motivated by evil.

6. **The correct answer is (4).** It is common for the title of a poem to also be the poem's first line. Regardless of the fact that the first line is also the title, choice (4) best summarizes the rest of the poem.

7. **The correct answer is (3).** This line, along with the rest of the passage, is describing a knight. Even if you couldn't see this based on the line, you can figure it out based on the rest of the passage.

8. **The correct answer is (4).** Throughout the passage, the author mentions and describes the extent to which the main character reads and reads about chivalry in particular.

9. **The correct answer is (1).** The first line of the last paragraph says that the main character's "wits were quite gone," meaning that he had gone crazy.

10. **The correct answer is (2).** A knight-errant is a knight who performs tasks or errands. The author specifically mentions tasks such as righting wrongs in the text.

11. **The correct answer is (3).** Based on the information in the passage, it is logical that the main character becomes a knight that sets out on a quest for adventures.

12. **The correct answer is (1).** The main character reads so much about knights and chivalry that he begins to believe that he is a knight-errant. His choice to become a knight-errant is influenced by the books he reads.

13. **The correct answer is (3).** The document introduces a new policy or procedure that is designed as a guideline for employees to follow regarding the time clock and time cards. It is the goal of the management to have no employees act inappropriately.

14. **The correct answer is (3).** Management has very carefully written the document in a very matter of fact, unemotional tone so employees are not offended or made uneasy by the memo.

15. **The correct answer is (5).** Based on the information in the memo, the most likely scenario is that the employees of the company have been careless or even deceptive in the past in their actions regarding the time clock and time card.

16. **The correct answer is (5).** All of the employees except for the accountant are employees who are paid by the hour or are non-salaried. The accountant, a professional, is most likely on salary. Because an accountant receives a salary, an accountant would not need to punch in and out. Therefore, the memo would not apply to an accountant.

17. **The correct answer is (4).** This line is a simile because it uses *like* to make a comparison.

18. **The correct answer is (2).** The images seen by the main character are merely imagined in the instant before he is hanged from a bridge.

19. **The correct answer is (1).** The first line of the passage indicates that he previously sustained some injury that caused him to suffer and fall asleep or pass out.

20. **The correct answer is (2).** The passage is in third person because the story is told by a narrator who observes the actions of the character and knows the thoughts and feelings of the character.

Day 26

Language Arts, Reading Practice Test (Part II)

For the purposes of this book, the Language Arts, Reading Test will be divided into two parts so that you will have time today and tomorrow to answer questions and review the answers in the amount of time you have allotted for GED preparation. For this practice test, give yourself 33 minutes to complete all the questions for Day 26. The GED Language Arts, Reading Test will contain 40 questions.

LANGUAGE ARTS, READING

Tests of General Educational Development Directions

The following are test directions reprinted by permission of the GED Testing Service.

The Language Arts, Reading Test consists of excerpts from fiction and nonfiction. Each excerpt is followed by multiple-choice questions about the reading material.

Read each excerpt first and then answer the questions following it. Refer back to the reading material as often as necessary in answering the questions.

Each excerpt is preceded by a "purpose question." The purpose question gives a reason for reading the material. Use these purpose questions to help focus your reading. You are not required to answer these purpose questions. They are given only to help you concentrate on the ideas presented in the reading material.

You will have 65 minutes to answer the 40 questions in this booklet. Work carefully, but do not spend too much time on any one question. Be sure that all requested information is properly recorded on the answer sheet.

Do not mark in this test booklet. Record your answers on the separate answer sheet provided. Be sure that all requested information is properly recorded on the answer sheet.

To record your answers, fill in the numbered circle on the answer sheet that corresponds to the answer you select for each question in the test booklet.

FOR EXAMPLE:

It was Susan's dream machine. The metallic blue paint gleamed, and the sporty wheels were highly polished. Under the hood, the engine was no less carefully cleaned. Inside, flashy lights illuminated the instruments on the dashboard, and the seats were covered by rich leather upholstery.

The subject (it) of this excerpt is most likely

(1) an airplane.

(2) a stereo system.

(3) an automobile.

(4) a boat.

(5) a motorcycle.

The correct answer is an automobile; therefore, answer space (3) would be marked on the answer sheet.

Do not rest the point of your pencil on the answer sheet while you are considering your answer. Make no stray or unnecessary marks. If you change an answer, erase your first mark completely. Mark only one answer space for each question; multiple answers will be scored as incorrect. Do not fold or crease your answer sheet. All test materials must be returned to the test administrator.

Directions: Items 1 to 6 are based on the following passage.

What are the author's feelings?

The traveling art exhibition "Italian Renaissance Masters" recently made a stop at the local university and gave local art enthusiasts an opportunity to witness some of the masterpieces of the Italian Renaissance without having to travel abroad. While many of the works of art took my breath away, the one work that stood out was the "David" by Michelangelo. The polished marble hero stood glistening in the lights of the museum hall as passersby stopped in awe. The colossal athletic figure spoke to all who stared in amazement. The gentle slopes and curves of his body, the incredible detail on his hands and feet, and the perfectly proportioned torso told a story of a craftsman who toiled for countless hours in search of perfection. The master had created a work of art that looked like it might step down from the pedestal at any moment. The figure looked like a Roman god. Every detail had been artfully considered. The hero's hair, cloak, and facial features all looked lightly delicate though they were made of solid marble. As I examined every detail of the masterpiece, I couldn't help but think that God himself must have created this perfect figure. I enjoyed all of the art and highly recommend the exhibit to everyone. However, I must suggest that you save the "David" for last as all other works of art simply pale in comparison.

21. Which of the following lines from the passage exemplifies the use of personification?

(1) "the works of art took my breath away"

(2) "The colossal athletic figure spoke to all"

(3) "other works of art simply pale in comparison"

(4) "The polished marble hero stood glistening"

(5) "The master had created a work of art"

22. The passage is most likely which of the following?

(1) A work of fiction

(2) An excerpt from a play

(3) A commentary

(4) An inter-office memo

(5) A persuasive essay

23. The figure referred to in the passage is most likely which of the following?

(1) A figure in a painting

(2) A model

(3) A character in a movie

(4) A sculptor

(5) A sculpture

24. The line "The figure looked like a Roman god" is an example of which of the following?

(1) Alliteration

(2) Simile

(3) Metaphor

(4) Personification

(5) Allegory

25. The overall mood or tone of the passage could best be described as which of the following?

    (1) Apprehensive

    (2) Reserved and stoic

    (3) Negative and condescending

    (4) Cautiously optimistic

    (5) Positive and laudatory

26. Which of the following best describes the author's feelings about what he saw at the exhibition?

    (1) The author was amazed at what he saw.

    (2) The author liked what he saw but was not too impressed.

    (3) The author would not recommend the exhibit to anyone else.

    (4) The author did not like any one thing more than another at the exhibit.

    (5) The author did not really express his feelings in the passage.

Directions: Items 27 to 30 are based on the following passage, an excerpt of Jane Austen's Pride and Prejudice.

What are Mr. Bingley and Mr. Darcy like?

Mr. Bingley was good-looking and gentlemanlike; he had a pleasant countenance, and easy, unaffected manners. His sisters were fine women, with an air of decided fashion. His brother-in-law, Mr. Hurst, merely looked the gentleman; but his friend Mr. Darcy soon drew the attention of the room by his fine, tall person, handsome features, noble mien, and the report which was in general circulation within five minutes after his entrance, of his having ten thousand a year. The gentlemen pronounced him to be a fine figure of a man, the ladies declared he was much handsomer than Mr. Bingley, and he was looked at with great admiration for about half the evening, till his manners gave a disgust which turned the tide of his popularity; for he was discovered to be proud; to be above his company, and above being pleased; and not all his large estate in Derbyshire could then save him from having a most forbidding, disagreeable countenance, and being unworthy to be compared with his friend.

Mr. Bingley had soon made himself acquainted with all the principal people in the room; he was lively and unreserved, danced every dance, was angry that the ball closed so early, and talked of giving one himself at Netherfield. Such amiable qualities must speak for themselves. What a contrast between him and his friend! Mr. Darcy danced only once with Mrs. Hurst and once with Miss Bingley, declined being introduced to any other lady, and spent the rest of the evening in walking about the room, speaking occasionally to one of his own party. His character was decided. He was the proudest, most disagreeable man in the world, and everybody hoped that he would never come there again. Amongst the most violent against him was Mrs. Bennet, whose dislike of his general behaviour was sharpened into particular resentment by his having slighted one of her daughters.

27. Which of the following caused Mr. Darcy's unpopularity?

    (1) His poor hygiene

    (2) His pride

    (3) His lack of money

    (4) His appearance

    (5) His shoddy clothes

28. Which of the following best describes the tone of the passage?

    (1) Harsh

    (2) Unbiased

    (3) Open-minded

    (4) Favorable

    (5) Positive

29. Which of the following is the setting of the passage?

    (1) A party

    (2) A sporting event

    (3) A funeral

    (4) A restaurant

    (5) A church

30. The line "He was the proudest, most disagreeable man in the world" is an example of which of the following?

    (1) Personification

    (2) Simile

    (3) Metaphor

    (4) Alliteration

    (5) Hyperbole

Directions: Items 31 to 36 are based on the following passage, an excerpt from William Shakespeare's **Romeo and Juliet.**

What is about to happen?

THE PROLOGUE [Enter Chorus.]

Chorus: Two households, both alike in dignity,

In fair Verona, where we lay our scene,

From ancient grudge break to new mutiny,

Where civil blood makes civil hands unclean.

From forth the fatal loins of these two foes

A pair of star-cross'd lovers take their life;

Whose misadventur'd piteous overthrows

Doth with their death bury their parents' strife.

The fearful passage of their death-mark'd love,

And the continuance of their parents' rage,

Which but their children's end naught could remove,

Is now the two hours' traffic of our stage;

The which, if you with patient ears attend,

What here shall miss, our toil shall strive to mend.

ACT I. Scene I. A public place. [Enter Sampson and Gregory armed with swords and bucklers.]

Sampson: Gregory, o' my word, we'll not carry coals.

Gregory: No, for then we should be colliers.

Sampson: I mean, an we be in choler we'll draw.

Gregory: Ay, while you live, draw your neck out o' the collar.

Sampson: I strike quickly, being moved.

Gregory: But thou art not quickly moved to strike.

Sampson: A dog of the house of Montague moves me.

Gregory: To move is to stir; and to be valiant is to stand: therefore, if thou art moved, thou runn'st away.

Sampson: A dog of that house shall move me to stand: I will take the wall of any man or maid of Montague's.

Gregory: That shows thee a weak slave; for the weakest goes to the wall.

Sampson: True; and therefore women, being the weaker vessels, are ever thrust to the wall: therefore I will push Montague's men from the wall and thrust his maids to the wall.

Gregory: The quarrel is between our masters and us their men.

Sampson: 'Tis all one, I will show myself a tyrant: when I have fought with the men I will be cruel with the maids, I will cut off their heads.

Gregory: The heads of the maids?

Sampson: Ay, the heads of the maids, or their maidenheads; take it in what sense thou wilt.

Gregory: They must take it in sense that feel it.

Sampson: Me they shall feel while I am able to stand: and 'tis known I am a pretty piece of flesh.

Gregory: 'Tis well thou art not fish; if thou hadst, thou hadst been poor-John.—Draw thy tool; Here comes two of the house of Montagues.

Sampson: My naked weapon is out: quarrel! I will back thee.

Gregory: How! turn thy back and run?

Sampson: Fear me not.

Gregory: No, marry; I fear thee!

Sampson: Let us take the law of our sides; let them begin.

Gregory: I will frown as I pass by; and let them take it as they list.

Sampson: Nay, as they dare. I will bite my thumb at them; which is disgrace to them if they bear it.

31. Which of the following is the setting of the passage?

    (1) A private residence in Verona

    (2) A public place in Padua

    (3) A church

    (4) A public place in Verona

    (5) A back room in the Montagues' home

32. Based on the passage, which of the following is the most likely purpose of the Chorus?

    (1) To sing a song before the play begins

    (2) To provide musical accompaniment

    (3) To inform the audience about things such as the setting

    (4) To interpret the play for the audience

    (5) To sing during intermission

33. In the line "Draw thy tool; Here comes two of the house of Montagues," the word *tool* means which of the following?

    (1) Hammer

    (2) Saw

    (3) Pen

    (4) Sword

    (5) Hand

34. In the line "Nay, as they dare. I will bite my thumb at them; which is disgrace to them if they bear it," which of the following is the best interpretation of the action of Sampson?

    (1) Sampson accidentally bit his own thumb.

    (2) Sampson will bite the thumbs of his enemies.

    (3) Sampson has made a disrespectful gesture.

    (4) Sampson is daring someone to bite his thumb.

    (5) Sampson has disgraced a bear.

35. Based on the information in the passage, which of the following is most likely to happen next in the play?

    (1) The two characters fight with one another.

    (2) The two characters have a confrontation with other characters from the house of Montague.

    (3) The two characters run away and hide.

    (4) The two characters befriend someone from the house of Montague.

    (5) The two characters continue to talk to each other.

36. Which of the following is the purpose of the prologue?

    (1) To briefly tell the story by telling the plot and giving away the ending

    (2) To allow the audience to get settled in their seats

    (3) To inform the audience of background information for the play

    (4) To tell the audience things that won't be presented during the play

    (5) To tell the audience what happens after the story

Directions: Items 37 to 40 are based on the following passage, an excerpt from Journey to the Interior of the Earth by Jules Verne.

On the 24th of May, 1863, my uncle, Professor Liedenbrock, rushed into his little house, No. 19 Konigstrasse, one of the oldest streets in the oldest portion of the city of Hamburg.

Martha must have concluded that she was very much behindhand, for the dinner had only just been put into the oven.

"Well, now," said I to myself, "if that most impatient of men is hungry, what a disturbance he will make!"

"M. Liedenbrock so soon!" cried poor Martha in great alarm, half opening the dining-room door.

"Yes, Martha; but very likely the dinner is not half cooked, for it is not two yet. Saint Michael's clock has only just struck half-past one."

"Then why has the master come home so soon?"

"Perhaps he will tell us that himself."

"Here he is, Monsieur Axel; I will run and hide myself while you argue with him."

And Martha retreated in safety into her own dominions.

I was left alone. But how was it possible for a man of my undecided turn of mind to argue successfully with so irascible a person as the Professor? With this persuasion I was hurrying away to my own little retreat upstairs, when the street door creaked upon its hinges; heavy feet made the whole flight of stairs to shake; and the master of the house, passing rapidly through the dining-room, threw himself in haste into his own sanctum.

But on his rapid way he had found time to fling his hazel stick into a corner, his rough broadbrim upon the table, and these few emphatic words at his nephew: "Axel, follow me!"

I had scarcely had time to move when the Professor was again shouting after me: "What! not come yet?" And I rushed into my redoubtable master's study.

Otto Liedenbrock had no mischief in him, I willingly allow that; but unless he very considerably changes as he grows older, at the end he will be a most original character.

He was professor at the Johannaeum, and was delivering a series of lectures on mineralogy, in the course of every one of which he broke into a passion once or twice at least. Not at all that he was over-anxious about the improvement of his class, or about the degree of attention with which they listened to him, or the success which might eventually crown his labours. Such little matters of detail never troubled him much. His teaching was as the German philosophy calls it, 'subjective'; it was to benefit himself, not others. He was a learned egotist. He was a well of science, and the pulleys worked uneasily when you wanted to draw anything out of it. In a word, he was a learned miser.

37. Which of the following is the setting of this passage?

(1) Twentieth-century Germany
(2) Nineteenth-century Germany
(3) Eighteenth-century Germany
(4) At the center of the earth in the nineteenth century
(5) At the center of the earth in the eighteenth century

38. In the line "Martha must have concluded that she was very much behindhand, for the dinner had only just been put into the oven," which of the following is the best meaning for *behindhand*?

(1) Without a hand
(2) In need of a hand
(3) Running behind schedule
(4) Hurting in her hands
(5) Behind closed doors

39. Which of the following is the best interpretation of the line "And Martha retreated in safety into her own dominions"?

(1) Martha locked herself in her room.
(2) Martha retreated to her own house where she was safe.
(3) Martha ran away.
(4) Martha moved to another country.
(5) Martha went back into the kitchen where she was most comfortable.

40. Which of the following best describes the professor?

(1) High strung and demanding
(2) Laid back and relaxed
(3) Dimwitted and confused
(4) Uneducated
(5) Harsh and bitter

Answer Explanations

21. **The correct answer is (2).** By saying that the figure, a sculpture, spoke to all, the author is using a literary technique called personification. In other words, the author gave human qualities to an inanimate object.

22. **The correct answer is (3).** The passage is a commentary or critique of an art exhibition and of a specific work of art in the exhibition.

23. **The correct answer is (5).** The figure described by the author is a very famous sculpture by the Renaissance artist Michelangelo. The sculpture is called "David."

24. **The correct answer is (2).** By saying the figure looked *like* a Roman god, the author is using a literary tool called a simile. A simile makes a comparison using *like* or *as*.

25. **The correct answer is (5).** The author uses language that gives much praise throughout the passage.

26. **The correct answer is (1).** The author expresses his wonder and amazement, especially about the statue, "David."

27. **The correct answer is (2).** Mr. Darcy's pride made everyone resent him.

28. **The correct answer is (1).** The language used to describe Mr. Darcy is very harsh and sets the tone for the entire passage.

29. **The correct answer is (1).** The setting of the passage is a ball or a large party, as indicated by the first line of the second paragraph.

30. **The correct answer is (5).** The line is a huge exaggeration, known in literature as a hyperbole.

31. **The correct answer is (4).** The play is set in Verona in a public place. Although this information isn't presented in the same place in the play, both *Verona* and *public place* are mentioned to the audience.

32. **The correct answer is (3).** The Chorus often acts as a narrator and informs the audience of things such as setting or background information.

33. **The correct answer is (4).** The word *tool* is used instead of the word *sword*.

34. **The correct answer is (3).** Sampson "bit his thumb at them" or made a disrespectful gesture at the members of the house of Montague.

35. **The correct answer is (2).** Based on the tone and the actions of the characters, it is logical that the characters have a fight with the members of the house of Montague whom they have just spotted.

36. **The correct answer is (3).** The prologue, which is found at the beginning of the work, gives background information that the audience will need to better understand the play.

37. **The correct answer is (2).** The setting is Germany, 1863. You can deduce this from the date, the German names, the mention of Hamburg, and the mention of German philosophy.

38. **The correct answer is (3).** Martha was running behind schedule because she had just put dinner in the oven, but the professor was ready to eat.

39. **The correct answer is (5).** Martha went back into the kitchen, her dominion, where she was in control and felt the most comfortable.

40. **The correct answer is (1).** The professor is portrayed as very high strung and very demanding of the people around him.

Day 27

Mathematics, Calculator Permitted Practice Test

BOOKLET ONE: MATHEMATICAL UNDERSTANDING AND APPLICATION

---

25 Questions—45 Minutes—Calculator Permitted

1. ① ② ③ ④ ⑤   7. ① ② ③ ④ ⑤   14. ① ② ③ ④ ⑤   20. ① ② ③ ④ ⑤
2. ① ② ③ ④ ⑤   8. ① ② ③ ④ ⑤   15. ① ② ③ ④ ⑤   24. ① ② ③ ④ ⑤
3. ① ② ③ ④ ⑤   11. ① ② ③ ④ ⑤   17. ① ② ③ ④ ⑤   25. ① ② ③ ④ ⑤
5. ① ② ③ ④ ⑤   12. ① ② ③ ④ ⑤   18. ① ② ③ ④ ⑤
6. ① ② ③ ④ ⑤   13. ① ② ③ ④ ⑤   19. ① ② ③ ④ ⑤

4.

	/	/	/	
.	.	.	.	.
0	0	0	0	0
1	1	1	1	1
2	2	2	2	2
3	3	3	3	3
4	4	4	4	4
5	5	5	5	5
6	6	6	6	6
7	7	7	7	7
8	8	8	8	8
9	9	9	9	9

9.

	/	/	/	
.	.	.	.	.
0	0	0	0	0
1	1	1	1	1
2	2	2	2	2
3	3	3	3	3
4	4	4	4	4
5	5	5	5	5
6	6	6	6	6
7	7	7	7	7
8	8	8	8	8
9	9	9	9	9

10.

16.

	/	/	/	
.	.	.	.	.
0	0	0	0	0
1	1	1	1	1
2	2	2	2	2
3	3	3	3	3
4	4	4	4	4
5	5	5	5	5
6	6	6	6	6
7	7	7	7	7
8	8	8	8	8
9	9	9	9	9

21.

	/	/	/	
.	.	.	.	.
0	0	0	0	0
1	1	1	1	1
2	2	2	2	2
3	3	3	3	3
4	4	4	4	4
5	5	5	5	5
6	6	6	6	6
7	7	7	7	7
8	8	8	8	8
9	9	9	9	9

22.

	/	/	/	
.	.	.	.	.
0	0	0	0	0
1	1	1	1	1
2	2	2	2	2
3	3	3	3	3
4	4	4	4	4
5	5	5	5	5
6	6	6	6	6
7	7	7	7	7
8	8	8	8	8
9	9	9	9	9

23.

	/	/	/	
.	.	.	.	.
0	0	0	0	0
1	1	1	1	1
2	2	2	2	2
3	3	3	3	3
4	4	4	4	4
5	5	5	5	5
6	6	6	6	6
7	7	7	7	7
8	8	8	8	8
9	9	9	9	9

MATHEMATICS

Tests of General Educational Development Directions

The following are test directions reprinted by permission of the GED Testing Service.

The Mathematics Test consists of questions intended to measure general mathematics skills and problem-solving ability. The questions are based on short readings that often include a graph, chart, or figure.

You will have 45 minutes to complete the 25 questions in this booklet. Work carefully, but do not spend too much time on any one question. Be sure you answer every question.

Formulas you may need are given on page 2. Only some of the questions will require you to use a formula. Not all the formulas given will be needed.

Some questions contain more information than you will need to solve the problem; other questions do not give enough information. If the question does not give enough information to solve the problem, the correct answer choice is "Not enough information is given."

The use of calculators is allowed.

Do not mark in this test booklet. Record your answers on the separate answer sheet provided. Be sure that all requested information is properly recorded on the answer sheet.

To record your answers, fill in the numbered circle on the answer sheet that corresponds to the answer you select for each question in the test booklet.

FOR EXAMPLE:

If a grocery bill totaling $15.75 is paid with a $20.00 bill, how much change should be returned?

(1) $5.25

(2) $4.75

(3) $4.25

(4) $3.75

(5) $3.25

The correct answer is $4.25; therefore, answer space (3) would be marked on the answer sheet.

Do not rest the point of your pencil on the answer sheet while you are considering your answer. Make no stray or unnecessary marks. If you change an answer, erase your first mark completely. Mark only one answer space for each question; multiple answers will be scored as incorrect. Do not fold or crease your answer sheet. All test materials must be returned to the test administrator.

Mathematics

Mixed numbers such as $3\frac{1}{2}$ cannot be entered in the alternate format grid. Instead, represent them as decimal numbers (in this case, 3.5) or fractions (in this case, 7/2). No answer can be a negative number, such as –8.

To record your answer for an alternate format question,

- begin in any column that will allow your answer to be entered;

- write your answer in the boxes on the top row;

- in the column beneath a fraction bar or decimal point (if any) and each number in your answer, fill in the bubble representing that character; and

- leave blank any unused column.

EXAMPLE:

The scale on a map indicates that 1/2 inch represents an actual distance of 120 miles. In inches, how far apart on the map will two towns be if the actual distance between them is 180 miles? The answer to the above example is 3/4, or 0.75 inches. A few examples of how the answer could be gridded are shown on the following page.

Points to remember:

- The answer sheet will be machine scored. **The circles must be filled in correctly.**

- Mark no more than one circle in any column.

- Grid only one answer, even if there is more than one correct answer.

- Mixed numbers such as $3\frac{1}{2}$ must be gridded as 3.5 or 7/2.

- No answer can be a negative number

CALCULATOR DIRECTIONS

To prepare the calculator for use the **first** time, press the **ON** (upper-rightmost) key. "DEG" will appear at the top-center of the screen as "0." at the right. This indicates the calculator is in the proper format for all your calculations.

To prepare the calculator for **another** question, press the **ON** or the red **AC** key. This clears any entries made previously.

To do any arithmetic, enter the expression as it is written. Press = (equals sign) when finished.

EXAMPLE A: 8–3+9

First press **ON** or **AC**

Enter the following: **8 – 3 + 9 =**

The correct answer is 14.

If an expression in parentheses is to be multiplied by a number, press × (multiplication sign) between the number and the parenthesis sign.

EXAMPLE B: 6(8+5)

First press **ON** or **AC**

Enter the following: **6 × (8 + 5) =**

The correct answer is 78.

To find the square root of a number,

- enter the number;

- press the **SHIFT** (upper-leftmost) key ("SHIFT" appears at top-left of the screen); and

- press x^2 (third from the left on top row) to access its second function: square root.

DO NOT press **SHIFT** and x^2 at the same time.

EXAMPLE C: $\sqrt{64}$

First press **ON** or **AC**

Enter the following: **6 4 SHIFT x^2 =**

The correct answer is 8.

To enter a negative number such as –8,

- enter the number without the negative sign (enter 8) and

- press the change sign (+/–) key, which is directly above the 7 key.

All arithmetic can be done with positive and/or negative numbers.

EXAMPLE D: –8 – –5
First press **ON** or **AC**
Enter the following: **8 +/– – 5 +/– =**
The correct answer is –3.

1. David packed a total of 40 boxes in 5 hours. How many boxes would Samuel have to pack in 3 hours in order to pack the same number of boxes?

   (1) 24
   (2) 25
   (3) 45
   (4) 15
   (5) 30

2. If 24 pencils cost $4.82, how much would 4 pencils cost?

   (1) $2.40
   (2) $.81
   (3) $.60
   (4) $1.20
   (5) $1.40

3. The prices of a gallon of milk at different grocery stores are $1.39, $1.22, $1.29, and $1.30. What is the average price of a gallon of milk?

   (1) $1.32
   (2) $1.31
   (3) $1.25
   (4) $1.29
   (5) $1.30

4. Mrs. Gabaway wants to telephone her friend in Boston. The day rate is $.48 for the first minute and $.34 for each additional minute. The evening rate discounts the day rate by 35 percent. If Mrs. Gabaway is planning a 45-minute chat, to the nearest penny, how much would she save if she took advantage of the evening rate by calling after 5 p.m.?

Mark your answer in the circles in the grid on your answer sheet.

5. $\sqrt{64} + 16 =$

   (1) 80
   (2) 48
   (3) 24
   (4) 32
   (5) 26

6. Melissa had $500 in her checking account. She wrote checks in the amounts of $35.75, $120.50, $98.25, and $350. She then deposited $375. How much money did she have in her account after her deposit?

   (1) $375
   (2) $270.50
   (3) $604.50
   (4) $200
   (5) Insufficient data is given to solve the problem.

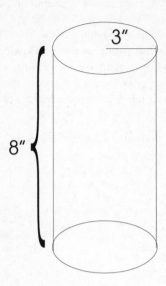

3"

8"

7. How many cubic inches of liquid can the cylindrical can above hold?

    (1) 48π

    (2) 64π

    (3) 96π

    (4) 72π

    (5) 108π

8. Find the value of $-6a + a^2 + 3(a + 6)$ if $a = 3$

    (1) -18

    (2) 27

    (3) 28

    (4) 18

    (5) 9

9. Jonathan drove his 66-year-old grandmother and 9-year-old little brother to the movie theater on Saturday afternoon. He treated all three of them to the matinee. The prices read as follows: Adults, $3.50; Children Under 12, $1.50; Senior Citizens, 20 percent discount. How much change did Jonathan receive from his $10.00 bill?

    Mark your answer in the circles in the grid on your answer sheet.

10. Quadrilateral ABCK is a square. The coordinates of point A are (3,2), the coordinates of point B are (–3,2), and the coordinates of point C are (–3,–4). On the coordinate plane on your answer sheet, mark the location of coordinate D.

11. Sarah has 25 dollars. She buys 2 books that cost 7 dollars and 50 cents each. How much money does she have left? Which expression represents this problem?

    (1) $x=25-7.50$

    (2) $x=25-2(7.50)$

    (3) $x=2(7.50)-25$

    (4) $2x=25-7.50$

    (5) Insufficient data is given to solve this problem.

12. What is the average height of a player on the 10th Street basketball team if the heights of the individual players are 5'8", 6'1", 5'10", 6'3", and 5'9"?

    (1) 5'8"

    (2) 5'9"

    (3) 5'11"

    (4) 5'10"

    (5) 6'

13. Sam returned a pair of shoes and was credited with $4.99 in his account. At the same store, he bought a shirt for $22.50, a tie for $14.95, and socks for $3.98. How much credit was remaining in his account?

    (1) $13.56

    (2) $13.00

    (3) $11.43

    (4) $12.50

    (5) $15.99

14. Ed bought his gasoline at a station that recently converted its pumps to measuring gasoline in liters. If his tank took 34.0 liters, approximately how many gallons did it take? One gallon is equal to 3.785 liters.

    (1) 9
    (2) 8
    (3) 9.25
    (4) 10
    (5) 11.5

15. At midnight, the temperature was –15°. By dawn, the temperature had risen 25°. What was the temperature at dawn?

    (1) 25°
    (2) –10°
    (3) 10°
    (4) –5°
    (5) –25°

16. Tom and Johnny leave the house at 6 a.m. to go camping. Colin decides to go with them, but to his dismay, when he reaches Tom's house, he learns that he and Johnny had left an hour ago. If Colin drives 65 MPH, how many hours will it take him to overtake his friends who are traveling at 45 MPH?

    Mark your answer in the circles in the grid on your answer sheet.

17. A college football team carried the ball 5 times in one quarter. During those 5 times, they gained 4 yards, lost 6 yards, lost 4 yards, gained 8 yards, and lost 5 yards. How many yards did they lose in all?

    (1) 11
    (2) 10
    (3) 5
    (4) 15
    (5) 3

18. Two ships leave the same harbor at the same time and travel in opposite directions, one at 30 km/hr and the other at 50 km/hr. After how many hours will they be 360 kilometers apart?

    (1) $2\frac{1}{2}$
    (2) $3\frac{1}{2}$
    (3) $5\frac{1}{2}$
    (4) $4\frac{1}{2}$
    (5) $6\frac{1}{2}$

19. In 1990, the average salary of a New Jersey teacher was $30,588. Ten years later, teachers in New Jersey were averaging $61,008. Find the nearest whole percentage of increase in salary from 1990 to 2000.

    (1) 99 percent
    (2) 100 percent
    (3) 50 percent
    (4) 86 percent
    (5) 75 percent

20. Juanita walked 1 hour 20 minutes every day for one full week. At the end of the week, how many hours did she walk altogether?

    (1) 7 hr. 20 min.
    (2) 8 hr.
    (3) 9 hr. 20 min.
    (4) 10 hr. 10 min.
    (5) Insufficient data is given to solve the problem.

21. In order to determine the expected mileage for a particular car, an automobile manufacturer conducts a factory test on five of these cars. The results, in miles per gallon, are 25.3, 23.6, 24.8, 23.0, and 24.3. What is the median mileage?

    Mark your answer in the circles in the grid on your answer sheet.

22. Stock in North American Electric fluctuated in price with a high of $67\frac{3}{4}$ and a low of $63\frac{5}{8}$. Find the difference between the high and the low price.

    Mark the answer in the circles in the grid on your answer sheet.

23. A woman bought 4 1/2 yards of ribbon to decorate curtains. If she cut the ribbon into 8 equal pieces, how long was each piece?

    Mark your answer in the circles in the grid on your answer sheet.

24. Thomas purchased 1 lb. 4 oz. bananas, 2 lb. 8 oz. apples, 3 lb. peaches, and 3 lb. 6 oz. plums. How much fruit did he buy?

    (1) 12 lb. 8 oz.

    (2) 10 lb. 2 oz.

    (3) 9 lb. 8 oz.

    (4) 10 lb. 8 oz.

    (5) 9 lb. 2 oz.

25. A discount toy store general takes $\frac{1}{5}$ off the list price of their merchandise. During the holiday season, an additional 15 percent is taken off the list price. Mrs. Johnson bought a sled listed at $62.00 for Joey and a dollhouse listed at $54.00 for Jill. To the nearest penny, how much did Mrs. Johnson pay?

    (1) $92.80

    (2) $78.88

    (3) $82.64

    (4) $75.40

    (5) $112.52

Answer Explanations

1. **The correct answer is (1).** Set up a grid to solve the problem. Multiply diagonally with known numbers, and then divide by the third known number.

boxes 40	?
hours 5	3

$40 \times 3 = 120$

$120 \div 5 = 24$

2. **The correct answer is (2).** Set up a grid to solve the problem. Multiply diagonally with known numbers, and then divide by the third known number.

pencils 24	4
cost $4.82	?

$\$4.82 \times 4 = \$19.28$

$\$19.28 \div 24 = \$0.81$

3. **The correct answer is (5).** Add $1.39, $1.22, $1.29, and $1.30, then divide by 4 (the number of items you added).

4. A day call would cost $0.34 × 44 minutes + $0.48, or $15.44. If the evening rate discounts the day rates by 35%, an evening call would cost 65% of $15.44, or 0.65×$15.44=$10.04. The savings is $15.44–$10.04, or $5.40. Therefore, the number $5.40 should be coded on your answer sheet, as shown below.

5. **The correct answer is (3).** The square root of 64 is 8 and 8+16=24.

6. **The correct answer is (2).** Add the amounts of the check written, subtract that number from the original $500.00 in the account, then add the deposit.

7. **The correct answer is (4).** The formula for the volume of a cylinder is $V = \pi r^2 h$. Thus, $V = \pi(3)^2(8) = \pi(9)(8) = 72\pi$.

8. **The correct answer is (4).**

$-6a + a^2 + 3(a+6) =$

$-6(3) + 9 + 3(9) =$

$-18 + 9 + 27 = 18$

9. If Jonathan drove, he must be an adult, so he paid $3.50 for his ticket and $1.50 for his brother's. His grandmother's ticket cost 80% of $3.50 = .8×3.50 = $2.80. Add the three ticket prices together and get $7.80. Jonathan got $2.20 in change. Therefore, the number $2.20 must be coded on your answer sheet.

10. When point A (3,2), and point B (–3,2), when connected, form a horizontal line segment of length 6, each side of the square must be length 6. The missing corner is 6 units below (3,2), which puts it at (3,–4). Therefore, the point (3,–4) must be entered on your answer sheet as shown below.

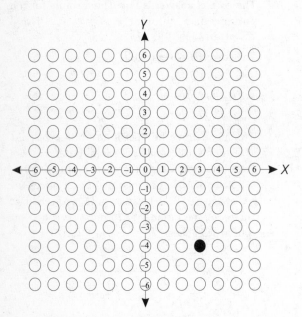

11. **The correct answer is (2).** $x = 25 – 2(7.50)25$ dollars is the original amount. Subtract the amount she spent on the books (2)(7.50).

12. **The correct answer is (3).** To find the average, add all the values given, then divide by the number of values. To add the values in this problem, first change all the heights to inches:

    5'8" = 68"

    6'1" = 73"

    5'10" = 70

    6'3" = 75"

    5'9" = 69"

    355" ÷ 5" = 71"

    71" ÷ 12" = 5'11"

13. **The correct answer is (1).** Add the amounts he spent. $22.50+$14.95+$3.98=$41.143. Subtract this amount from the total credit.

    $54.99–$41.43=$13.56.

14. **The correct answer is (1).** Divide 34.0 by 3.875 to get 8.98, which is closest to 9 liters.

15. **The correct answer is (3).** Add +25 (the amount the temperature rose) to –15 (the temperature at midnight).

16. Recall that $D=rt$.

    Colin and his friends travel the same distance, but Colin travels for 1 hour less than his friends.

    Let t = the number of hours Tom and Johnny travel.

    Then, $t–1$ = the number of hours Colin travels.

    $45t=65(t–1)$

    $45t=65t–65$

    $–20t= –65$

    $t=3\frac{1}{4}$ hours

    $t–1=2\frac{1}{4}$ hours. Thus, it will take Colin 2.25 hours to catch up to his friends. The answer must be coded on the answer sheet as shown below.

2	.	2	5	
	/	/	/	
•	●	•	•	•
0	0	0	0	0
1	1	1	1	1
●	2	●	2	2
3	3	3	3	3
4	4	4	4	4
5	5	5	●	5
6	6	6	6	6
7	7	7	7	7
8	8	8	8	8
9	9	9	9	9

17. **The correct answer is (5).** Add the yardage gained 4+8=12. Add the yardage lost (–6)+(–4)+(–5)= –15. Subtract the gain from the loss. Because the lost yardage is the greatest number, the answer is –3.

18. **The correct answer is (4).** Recall that $D=rt$. Since the two ships are moving in opposite directions, we may imagine one ship to be standing still and the other ship moving away from it at their combined rates of 80km/hr. In that case,

$D=rt$

$360=80t$

$t=4\frac{1}{2}$ hours

19. **The correct answer is (1).** The percent of increase in salary is computed by

$$\frac{61,008-30,588}{30,588}=\frac{30,420}{30,588}=0.9945=99.45\% \text{ or } 99\%.$$

20. **The correct answer is (3).** Multiply 1 hour 20 minutes times 7 = 7 hours 140 minutes. Convert 140 minutes into hours. 140 ÷ 60=2 hours 20 minutes. Add the converted hours to the answer = 9 hours 20 minutes.

21. The median mileage is simply the mileage in the middle when the 5 mileages are written in numerical order. This number is 24.3. Therefore, 24.3 must be coded on the answer sheet as shown below:

2	4	.	3	
	/	/	/	
•	•	●	•	•
0	0	0	0	0
1	1	1	1	1
●	2	2	2	2
3	3	3	●	3
4	●	4	4	4
5	5	5	5	5
6	6	6	6	6
7	7	7	7	7
8	8	8	8	8
9	9	9	9	9

22. $67\frac{3}{4}-63\frac{5}{8}=67\frac{6}{8}-63\frac{5}{8}=4\frac{1}{8}=4.125.$

Therefore, the number 4.125 must be coded on the answer sheet as shown below:

4	.	1	2	5
	/	/	/	
•	●	•	•	•
0	0	0	0	0
1	1	●	1	1
2	2	2	●	2
3	3	3	3	3
●	4	4	4	4
5	5	5	5	●
6	6	6	6	6
7	7	7	7	7
8	8	8	8	8
9	9	9	9	9

23. Divide $4\frac{1}{2}$ by 8: $4.5 \div 8 = 0.5625$. This answer must be coded onto your answer sheet as shown below.

.	5	6	2	5
	/	/	/	
●	•	•	•	•
0	0	0	0	0
1	1	1	1	1
2	2	2	●	2
3	3	3	3	3
4	4	4	4	4
5	●	5	5	●
6	6	●	6	6
7	7	7	7	7
8	8	8	8	8
9	9	9	9	9

24. **The correct answer is (2).** 1 lb. 4 oz. + 2 lb. 8 oz. + 3 lb. 6 oz. = 9 lb. 18 oz. Convert to 10 lb. 2 oz.

25. **The correct answer is (4).** $\frac{1}{5}$ is 20%. If both are taken off the list price, then the discount is actually 35%. The total purchases are $116. If 35% is coming off that, then 65% is being paid. .65(116) = $75.40.

Day 28

Mathematics, Calculator Not Permitted Practice Test

BOOKLET TWO: ESTIMATION AND MENTAL MATH

25 Questions—45 Minutes—Calculator Not Permitted

1. ① ② ③ ④ ⑤
2. ① ② ③ ④ ⑤
3. ① ② ③ ④ ⑤
4. ① ② ③ ④ ⑤
5. ① ② ③ ④ ⑤
6. ① ② ③ ④ ⑤
7. ① ② ③ ④ ⑤
8. ① ② ③ ④ ⑤
9. ① ② ③ ④ ⑤
10. ① ② ③ ④ ⑤
12. ① ② ③ ④ ⑤
13. ① ② ③ ④ ⑤
14. ① ② ③ ④ ⑤
16. ① ② ③ ④ ⑤
18. ① ② ③ ④ ⑤
19. ① ② ③ ④ ⑤
20. ① ② ③ ④ ⑤
21. ① ② ③ ④ ⑤
22. ① ② ③ ④ ⑤
23. ① ② ③ ④ ⑤
24. ① ② ③ ④ ⑤
25. ① ② ③ ④ ⑤

11.

15.

17.

1. Mona bought 2 packages of ground beef, each weighing 3 pounds 4 ounces, and a package of pork chops weighing 2 pounds 9 ounces. How many pounds of meat did she buy?

   (1) 5 pounds 13 ounces

   (2) 9 pounds

   (3) 9 pounds 1 ounce

   (4) 6 pounds 9 ounces

   (5) 8 pounds 9 ounces

2. Mr. Jackson has a pine board measuring 8 ft. 5 in. and a redwood board measuring 6 ft. 8 in. How much larger is the pine board than the redwood board?

   (1) 1 ft. 9 in.

   (2) 2 ft. 3 in.

   (3) 2 ft. 9 in.

   (4) 2 ft.

   (5) 1 ft. 3 in.

3. Find the value of x in the equation $x+3x+(x+3)=18$.

   (1) 4

   (2) 3

   (3) 2

   (4) 5

   (5) 6

4. There were only 8 inches of snowfall in 1993 in Laketown and 24 inches the following year. What is the ratio of snowfall from 1993 to 1994?

   (1) 8:24

   (2) 24:8

   (3) 3:1

   (4) 8:32

   (5) 1:3

5. A plumber completed five jobs yesterday. On the first job, she earned $36.45, the second $52.80, the third $42.81, the fourth $49.54, and the fifth $48.90. What was the average amount she earned for each job?

   (1) $38.50

   (2) $39.75

   (3) $40.80

   (4) $46.10

   (5) $42.50

6. Henry's VW Rabbit Diesel gets 50 mpg. Diesel fuel costs an average of $1.10 per gallon. This summer, Henry and his family drove 1,200 miles to Niagara Falls for vacation. How much did Henry pay for fuel?

   (1) $52.80

   (2) $26.40

   (3) $105.60

   (4) $132.20

   (5) $264.00

7. Lili bought 3 quarts of soda to make punch for a party. If she had 3 pints left over, how much did she use?

   (1) 1 quart

   (2) 2 quarts

   (3) 3 pints

   (4) 2 pints

   (5) 1 pint

Top Purchasers of U.S. Exports

1999
Total U.S. Exports – $510 Billion

2000
Total U.S. Exports – $575 Billion

8. How much more did Germany spend on U.S. exports than Taiwan in 2000?

   (1) $5.75 billion
   (2) $17.25 billion
   (3) $23 billion
   (4) $2.3 billion
   (5) $575,000,000

9. Approximately how much money did the United Kingdom spend on the purchase of U.S. exports in 1999?

   (1) $31 billion
   (2) $3.1 billion
   (3) $29 billion
   (4) $2.9 billion
   (5) $33 billion

10. How many countries spent more than $25 billion for U.S. exports in 2000?

    (1) 2
    (2) 3
    (3) 8
    (4) 6
    (5) 4

11. Consider the equation $y = 7x - 3$. On the grid on your answer page, mark the y-intercept of this equation.

12. Jackie is leaving from New York on a flight to Los Angeles at 1:30 p.m.. The flight takes 4 hours 30 minutes, and she will lose 3 hours of time by traveling to the West Coast. What time will she arrive in Los Angeles?

    (1) 2:30 p.m.
    (2) 6:00 p.m.
    (3) 5:00 p.m.
    (4) 3:00 p.m.
    (5) 5:30 p.m.

13. On a map, 1 inch represents 3 miles. How many inches are needed to represent a road that is actually 171 miles long?

    (1) 513 inches
    (2) 57 inches
    (3) 121 inches
    (4) 3 inches
    (6) 17 inches

14. A coat that lists for $240 is on sale for $180. By what percent has the coat been discounted?

    (1) 40 percent

    (2) 35 percent

    (3) 25 percent

    (4) 30 percent

    (5) 20 percent

15. The snail can creep at speeds up to 0.03 mph, but the snail has also been observed to travel as slowly as 0.0036 mph. Find the difference between the snail's fastest and slowest speeds.

    Mark your answer in the circles in the grid on your answer sheet.

16. The diameter of a circular playground is 60 feet. If Anthony walks around the playground twice, how many feet will he have walked?

    (1) 376.8 ft.

    (2) 120 ft.

    (3) 300.8 ft.

    (4) 188.4 ft.

    (5) 326.7 ft.

17. In right triangle DEF below, what is the value of tan D?

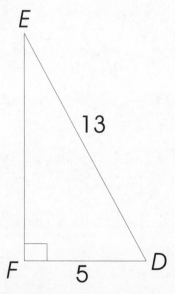

Mark your answer in the circles in the grid on your answer sheet.

18. 527(3–6 + 274) has the same value as which of the following?

    (1) 316(527) + 274

    (2) 316 + 527 + 274

    (3) 527(274 + 316(274)

    (4) 316(527) + 316(274)

    (5) 527(316) + 527(274)

19. Twice the sum of 3 and a number is 1 less than 3 times the number. If the letter N is used to represent the number, which of the following equations could be solved in order to determine the number?

    (1) $2(3) + N = 3N - 1$

    (2) $2(3 + N) = 3N - 1$

    (3) $2(3 \times N) = 3N - 1$

    (4) $2(3 + N) - 1 = 3N$

    (5) $2(3 + N) = 1 - 3N$

20. Over a six-month period, a certain stock rose 6 points, fell 4 points, fell another 8 points, rose 5 points for each of the next two months, and ended the period by rising another 3 points. What was the total gain for this stock?

    (1) 4 points

    (2) 2 points

    (3) 19 points

    (4) 7 points

    (5) 6 points

21. The sailfish is built for speed and can swim through the water at speeds of 68 mph. Approximately how many kilometers can it travel in an hour? 1 kilometer = .62 miles.

    (1) 109 km/hr.

    (2) 68 km/hr.

    (3) 96 km/hr.

    (4) 110 km/hr.

    (5) 42 km/hr.

22. If $x^2 + 5x + 6 = 0$ then $x =$
    (1) +3 and +2
    (2) –3 only
    (3) –2 and –3
    (4) +5 only
    (5) +2 only

23. James plans to cut 58 meters of fencing into 8 pieces of equal length. How long will each piece be?
    (1) 464 meters
    (2) 7.5 meters
    (3) 8 meters
    (4) 64 meters
    (5) 7.25 meters

24. There are 155 children signed up for a class field trip. The number of girls exceeds the number of boys by 17. If B represents the number of boys, which of the following equations could be solved to determine the number of boys signed up for the class trip?
    (1) B + (B –17) = 155
    (2) B + (B + 17) = 155
    (3) 155 + B = B + 17
    (4) 155 + B = B – 17
    (5) B + (B – 17) = 138

25. A vending machine contains $21 in dimes and nickels. Altogether, there are 305 coins. If N represents the number of nickels, which of the following equations could be solved in order to determine the value of N?
    (1) .10(N – 305) + .5N = 21
    (2) 10(305 – N) + 5N = 21
    (3) .10N + .05(305 – N) = 21
    (4) .10(305 – N) + .05n = 21
    (5) .10(N – 21) + 5N = 305

Answer Explanations

1. **The correct answer is (3).** Add 3 lb. 4 oz., 3 lb. 4 oz., 2 lb. 9 oz. = 8 lb. 17 oz. Convert the 17 oz. to pounds and add to the answer = 9 lb. 1 oz.

2. **The correct answer is (1).** Convert 8 ft. 5 in. to 7 ft. 17 in. 7 ft. 17 in. − 6 ft. 8 in. = 1 ft. 9 in.

3. **The correct answer is (2).** $x + 3x + (x + 3) = 18$

   $5x + 3 = 18$

   $5x = 18 - 3$

   $5x = 15$

   $x = \dfrac{15}{5}$

   $x = 3$

4. **The correct answer is (5).** The ratio of snowfall from 1993 to 1994 is 8:24. Reduced to the lowest terms, the ratio is 1:3.

5. **The correct answer is (4).** To find the average, add all the values given, then divide by the number of values.

6. **The correct answer is (2).** 1200 miles ÷ 50 miles = 24 gallons used. Then multiply $1.10 by 24 to get a total cost of $26.40.

7. **The correct answer is (3).** Convert 3 quarts to 6 pints, then subtract 3 pints = 3 pints.

8. **The correct answer is (1).** Germany spent $575 billion × .04 = $23 billion. Taiwan spent $575 billion × .03 = 17.25 billion. The difference is 23 − 17.25 = $5.75 billion.

9. **The correct answer is (1).** The United Kingdom purchased 6% of $510 billion = $510 billion × .06 = $30.6 billion, which is closest to $31 billion.

10. **The correct answer is (5).** The quickest way to answer this problem is to find what percent $25 billion is of $575 billion. Since 25 ÷ 575 = 0.043 = 4.3%. So, any country that purchases more than 4.3% of the U.S. exports would have spent more than $25 billion. There are 4 such countries: Canada, Japan, Mexico, and the United Kingdom.

11. The given equation, $y = 7x - 3$, is already in the slope-intercept form. Therefore, the y-intercept is at −3, that is, at the point (0,−3). The grid should be filled in as shown.

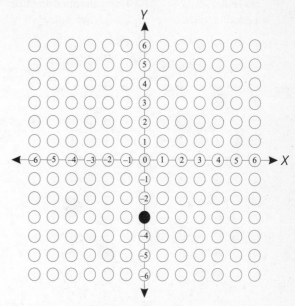

12. **The correct answer is (4).** 1:30 + 4 hr. 30 min. = 6:00. Subtract 3 hours for the time difference. 6:00 − 3 hr. = 3:00.

13. **The correct answer is (2).** A proportion can be established between the scale of the map in inches and the actual distance in miles:

    $\dfrac{1}{3} = \dfrac{x}{171}$

    $3x = 171$

    $x = 57$ inches

14. **The correct answer is (3).** Make a proportion:

    $\dfrac{180}{240} = \dfrac{x}{100}$

    $\dfrac{3}{4} = \dfrac{x}{100}$

    $4x = 300$

    $x = 75\%$

    Because x is 75% of the original price, the original price has been reduced by 25%.

15. Since 0.03-0.0036 = 0.0264, this number must be coded on the answer grid, as shown below.

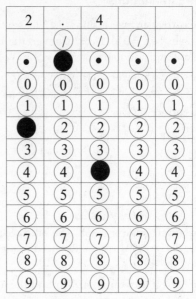

16. **The correct answer is (4).**

$C = \pi d$

C=3.14 × 60

C=188.4

17. To begin, find the length of the missing side *EF* by using the Pythagorean Theorem:

$(EF)^2 + 5^2 = 13^2$

$(EF)^2 + 25 = 169$

$(EF)^2 = 144$

$EF = 12$

Since the tangent of an angle is the ratio $\dfrac{opposite}{adjacent}$, compute tan D = $\dfrac{12}{5}$. Since this is equal to 2.4, this number must be coded onto your answer sheet as shown.

18. **The correct answer is (5).** This is an illustration of the distributive property.

527(316+274)=527(316)+527(274)

19. **The correct answer is (2).** The word *sum* indicates addition, so twice the sum of 3 and a number is represented by 2(3+N). Then, *less than* indicates subtraction, so 1 less than 3 times the number is by 3N–1.

20. **The correct answer is (4).** 6+5+5+3=19 These four figures represent the months in which the stock rose. (–4) + (–8) = (–12) These two figures represent the months in which the stock fell. (+19) + (–12) = +7

21. **The correct answer is (4).** Since a kilometer is less than a mile, it will travel more than 68 kilometers. Multiplying by a fraction (.62) will give a smaller number, so we must divide $\dfrac{68}{.62}$ =109.67=110 kilometers.

22. **The correct answer is (3).**

    $x^2 + 5x + 6 = 0$

    $(x+3)(x+2) = 0$

    $x+3 = 0$ or $x+2 = 0$

    $x = -3$ or $x = -2$

23. **The correct answer is (5).**

    $\dfrac{58}{8} = 7.25$ meters

24. **The correct answer is (2).** If B represents the number of boys, then the number of girls would be represented by B + 17. Since the number of girls plus the number of boys totals 155, it must be true that B + (B + 17) = 155.

25. **The correct answer is (4).** If N represents the number of nickels, then the number of dimes must be 305–N. Each nickel is worth $0.05, so the total value of the nickels in the machine is .05N. Similarly, the total value of the dimes in the machine is .10(305–N). The value of the nickels plus the value of the dimes added together is $21, so .10(305–N) + .05N = 21.

Day 29 to Day 30

Review of Strategies and Final Suggestions

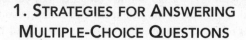

Day 29

Review of Test-Taking Strategies

Topics for today:

1. Strategies for Answering Multiple-Choice Questions
2. Strategies for Answering Questions about Reading Passages
3. Strategies for Answering Questions about Visuals
4. Strategies for Better Writing
5. General Test-Taking Strategies

1. STRATEGIES FOR ANSWERING MULTIPLE-CHOICE QUESTIONS

Let's briefly review some strategies for answering multiple-choice questions. First, read the question carefully and make sure you know what the question is asking. Read the question slowly, run your pencil under the sentence, or even underline key words so you don't misunderstand the question. Second, don't over-analyze the question or read something into the question that just isn't there. Take the question at face value. Third, after you read the question, try to answer the question in your head before you look at the answer choices. If you have the answer to the question in your head, you will easily spot the correct answer among the answer choices. You may also want to try covering the answer choices while you are reading the question. Fourth, carefully read all the answer choices before answering the question. Even if you think you see the correct answer early on, read all the answer choices just to make sure. Eliminate those answer choices that you know are wrong. When you find

the right answer, go with your first answer. Also, don't go back and change your answer unless you have a good, solid reason to do so. Next, don't spend too much time on one question. You need to pace yourself, so don't get bogged down on one question. Finally, if you don't know the correct answer, guess. There is no penalty for guessing, so take a shot at the question. You have nothing to lose.

2. STRATEGIES FOR ANSWERING QUESTIONS ABOUT READING PASSAGES

Let's go back over a few of the most important things to remember as you read the passages and documents on the tests. First, look for the topic sentence of each paragraph. Often the topic sentence is the first sentence in a paragraph. However, occasionally the topic sentence will be the last sentence of a paragraph. Second, if you read several paragraphs, consider the main idea of the entire document. The main idea is the general point of the document. Finally, consider things such as who the author is, the author's point of view, the intended audience, and whether or not the author has written the document as fact or fiction. These things will help you answer all sorts of questions about the passage or document.

3. STRATEGIES FOR ANSWERING QUESTIONS ABOUT VISUALS

Let's review the strategies for questions about visuals. To answer questions about visuals, you'll need to correctly interpret the visuals. First, whether the visual is a map, a graph, a chart, or a cartoon, look carefully at the title or the caption. The title or caption will offer clues as to the meaning of the visual. If the visual is a map, use the map key or legend to decipher the symbols used on the map. If the visual is a cartoon, look for any recognizable people, places, or things within the cartoon that may offer clues. Also, look at the action or dialogue within the cartoon for clues. If the visual is a chart or graph, use the text that is given along the sides and across the top or bottom of the visual.

4. STRATEGIES FOR BETTER WRITING

The most important thing to remember when writing for the GED is that your writing should be clear, concise, and well organized. There are a few things to remember to help you do these things. First, organize your thoughts before you begin writing instead of just writing off the top of your head. Second, formulate a five-paragraph essay with an introductory paragraph, three supporting paragraphs, and a conclusion. Third, keep each paragraph simple and focused on the main idea or point you are trying to make. You should probably keep the main idea in the first sentence of each paragraph. Finally, don't ramble or add excess information. Keep it simple and get to the point. You should also remember to concentrate on spelling and grammar to add credibility to your writing.

5. GENERAL TEST-TAKING STRATEGIES

Let's go back over a few of the most important test-taking strategies that you should remember as you prepare for and take the GED Tests. First, don't try to cram all the GED Tests in a short period of time. You don't take the tests all at once, and you don't even have to take them all in one week. Spread out the test dates so that you have adequate time to prepare for each one. Second, make sure you are well rested and well fed before you take the test. You will be more alert and your memory will be better if you are not tired or hungry during the tests. Third, relax and don't be nervous before or during the tests. One thing you might try to help you relax is chewing gum during the test. This is a proven stress relief technique that may help you relieve anxiety. You have worked hard and are ready for the tests.

Here are a few things to keep in mind during the tests. First, take your time and don't rush through the tests. At the same time, though, pace yourself and don't spend too much time on one question. Second, read everything very carefully. Read the documents carefully, read the questions carefully, and read the answer choices carefully. Be sure to underline keywords in whatever you read so that you can find the important ideas if you need to refer back to what you read. Finally, simply do the best you can. You don't need a perfect score on any of the tests to receive a passing score.

Day 30

Final Suggestions Before You Take the Tests

Topics for today:

1. Knowing you are ready for the GED Tests
2. A few more suggestions
3. Final thoughts before you take the GED Tests

1. KNOWING YOU ARE READY FOR THE GED TESTS

If you have been diligent in working through this book for thirty days now, give yourself a hand and pat yourself on the back! You have gone far beyond taking the first step toward getting your GED credentials. For thirty days now, you have made a commitment to preparing yourself for the GED, and it is almost time for that commitment to pay off for you. Perhaps you have learned a great deal of new information and new skills during these thirty days, or perhaps you have simply brushed up on some knowledge and skills that you have been using for years. Either way, by working through this book, you have given yourself the boost you will need to be successful on the GED Tests. Maybe you are still asking yourself, "Am I really ready?" If you have worked through the book, if you remember the information, and if you use the strategies presented in this book, then you are ready for the tests.

2. A FEW MORE SUGGESTIONS

In the final days before you begin the GED Tests, consider these few last suggestions. Any of these suggestions that you can put into practice will help you be physically and mentally ready for the GED. First, in the few days leading up to each of the tests, try to avoid stressful situations. You will want to be relaxed and focused as you head into each test. Second, make sure that you get plenty of sleep in the days before each test. Don't stay up all night or even until the wee hours of the morning trying to cram for the tests. You have already put in the time to prepare; cramming will not help and may make you tired for the tests. Third, when you go to the testing center to take each test, make plans to arrive several minutes early. If you get stuck in traffic, get turned around on a school campus, or if you encounter some other unexpected delay, you won't be rushed if you allow yourself plenty of time to get to the test site. Finally, after you complete each test, don't spend time worrying or wondering how you did.

Take your test, move on, and begin final preparations for the next test. Worrying will not change anything, and it will keep you from maintaining your focus.

3. FINAL THOUGHTS BEFORE YOU TAKE THE GED TESTS

As you make your final preparations for the GED Tests, remember these few final thoughts. First, be proud of yourself for making the effort to prepare yourself the way you have these last thirty days. Take that pride with you into each of the tests and let that help motivate you if you begin to get tired or frustrated. Second, view the test-taking experience as a challenge instead of a chore. You have worked to prepare yourself for the GED; now it is time to put your preparation to the test. An athlete prepares so he can compete and meet challenges. The same holds true for you regarding the GED. Third, be confident in your abilities. You know what to expect, you know how to handle whatever the GED gives you, and you are ready. Finally, consider the rewards you will reap for your hard work. Perhaps you are completing the GED to get a promotion at work or to complete college prerequisites. Either way, you are giving yourself a chance to take advantage of a whole world of opportunities that you have not had before. Do a terrific job on each and every one of the tests and enjoy the feeling you surely will have when you receive your passing scores. Congratulations!

Notes

Notes

Notes

Notes

Notes

Notes

Your online ticket to educational and professional success!

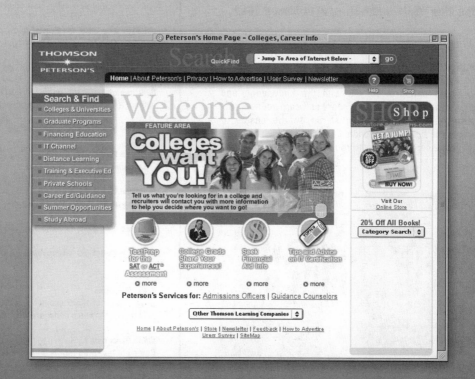

At **petersons.com**, *you can explore thousands of colleges, graduate programs, and distance learning programs; take online practice tests; and search the Internet's largest scholarship database and you'll find career advice you can use—tips on resumes, job-search strategies, interviewing techniques and more.*

www.petersons.com ■ tel: 800.338.3282

THOMSON

PETERSON'S

Hit the Books!